The Missin
the advanced seeker's gu

Eileen Watkins S...
with Clive Digby-Jones & Susan Norman

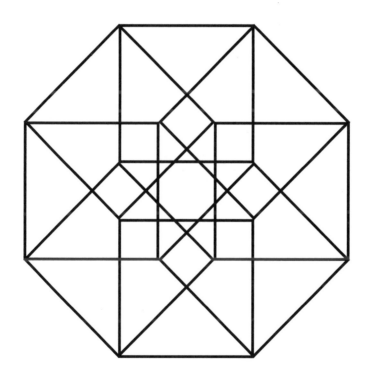

Saffire
PRESS

First published December 2003

Published by
Saffire Press
37 Park Hall Road
East Finchley
London N2 9PT
England
Fax +44(0)20 8444 0339
Email books@saffirepress.co.uk
www.saffirepress.co.uk

Design, including the cover, by Susan Norman and Hugh L'Estrange
Printed in Great Britain by Ashford Colour Press, Gosport, Hants

ISBN 1 901564 053

Introduction

Eileen Watkins Seymour was one of the first people to introduce Neuro-Linguistic Programming to the UK in the late 1970s. NLP is a theory of excellence. It looks for the 'difference that makes the difference' between people who are excellent in their field and the rest of us. It was based on modelling (copying exactly) therapists such as Milton Erickson and Virginia Satir who were having above average results with their clients. Modelling involves identifying the way the model structures their internal universe (the ways in which they think, act and react naturally), as well as how this is exemplified in their behaviour, and comparing this with other possible ways of thinking and behaving. This led to various understandings, such as the way each of us is made up of 'parts' which seem to act independently of one another, frequently in conflict with one another, and often they seem to be totally unaware of the existence of one another.

NLP is good. It is more than good. It works quickly and elegantly. It can cure, resolve or alleviate many problems which can take years in conventional therapy. However, Eileen began intuitively to take the practice further. To take a computing metaphor, if NLP is working at the level of software, Eileen was making profound changes to the operating system.

She called her new way of working 'wholistic NLP', then the 'Ravenscroft Approach' (named after the therapy centre and road in which she was living and working with her partner, Clive), then the 'Ravenscroft Approach to Psycho-Spiritual Integration' – and hence RAPSI. The practice develops and becomes more elegant all the time as each new person begins the fascinating exploration of their own internal universe. However, after working with nearly 2000 clients, and having seen the successes that trainee RAPSI practitioners have achieved, Eileen and Clive are now in a position to explain what they do and how it seems to work.

One thing they have noticed is that clients tend to come to them 'when the time is right' for each of them to take significant steps in their development. If you are reading this book now, it is because your own system knows that it is the right time for you to make progress.

Enjoy the journey.

This book is dedicated to
Mom and Dad on the other side,
to our children,
and to the light of all of us

*When I learnt the RAPSI message I knew that I had to help birth this book.
There are many models which talk about enlightenment,
but this is the first process which actually tells you how to get there.*

Eileen and Clive, it's been a privilege working with you.

Susan

Contents

That from which
Through which
In which
May be found all things,
Out of which all things come.
Thus, the first of everything
That may be visible in Earth,
In Heaven, in Space,
Is of that Light
Is that Light

Edgar Cayce

Chapter One

The human story

'Einstein showed that a human body contains enough energy trapped in its atoms to explode with a force of thirty of the largest thermo nuclear bombs'

From Bryson's *A Short History of Nearly Everything*

Everything is energy and comes from a divine source. There is a continuum of energy which vibrates at different frequencies from the most subtle dimensions to the physical world of matter. We too are made of this divine energy, some of which manifests as the physical body and some of which is vibrating at a different frequency, as part of the metaphysical dimensions.

As we go through our life, and lives, we have positive and negative experiences. While the positive experiences encourage us to radiate and express ourselves fully in the world, negative experiences initiate a withdrawing of energy. If the negative experience is intense enough, or if it is repeated enough times, our energy implodes and separates, and parts of us seem to shut down. In the place of radiance we have a fragmented energetic structure, which underpins and creates what happens to us in the physical dimension.

The intention is that if a part of us is shut down, it/we can't be hurt again. But although our system is trying to protect itself, and is therefore acting with entirely positive intent, the result is that we are not 'firing on all cylinders', we are 'not all here', and we are hurt by being less than we could be. Tension and struggle results.

And it is not just one part of us that shuts down. Over time at different stages of our lives, more of our energy splits off and becomes hidden, and each fragment covers itself with layers of protection.The result is that our energetic structure is like a multi-dimensional jigsaw puzzle which needs to be reunited so that it can radiate freely once again.

Sometimes we are conscious of what has hurt us in the past and we are aware that as a result we are shy, timid, fearful, self-conscious, lacking in confidence, lacking in self-esteem, unable to commit to a relationship, or that we compensate by over-eating, smoking, taking drugs, or by being loud, aggressive, naughty, or whatever. More often we just assume that that is 'how we are' as part of our genetic inheritance without considering our deeper 'energetic inheritance'.

You do not have to have suffered serious abuse for this fragmentation to occur. If you've been born and had a childhood, then you've been affected, the question is just one of degree. And because everyone is in the same boat, there is unconscious collusion between us. A certain level of not-coping is considered normal and acceptable, it can even be seen as attractive by some – or reassuring, since we seem to be doing quite well in comparison with other people. But this syndrome is leading to dysfunctional individuals in a dysfunctional society, where more and more people are quite obviously yearning for what they don't have and they are acting out their unhappiness and suffering. The external universe mirrors the internal.

In days gone by you were just expected to get on with it. 'You've made your bed, now lie in it.' 'Pull your socks up.' Now some of us are aware that we need help. More and more are turning to therapists of various kinds, the self-help books are leaping off bookstore shelves, and the 'mind, body, spirit' section grows ever larger. Others are so overwhelmed that they have given up all sense of responsibility for themselves and look to the state or charities or litigation payments to bale them out.

The message of this book is that it doesn't have to be like this. There is a better way. The RAPSI approach is not only for people who know there is something wrong in their lives and are taking personal responsibility to resolve their issues, it is also for those who are materially successful and who want to achieve more, want to be whole. You do not have to have broken down before you set out on your inner journey, a journey which we believe all of us needs to take if we want to grow and evolve.

You can do some of this with other therapies. Some of them take years. Some may encourage dependence on the therapist. Some can be quite distressing as they involve reliving traumatic experiences, sometimes repeatedly. Some though are positive and faster and seem to work. You may have experienced some of them. Each may bring you a piece of the puzzle, but what is important is to discover the underlying structure, the origin of the problem, the big picture.

So what are you still looking for? What is the missing piece – your missing peace about? What does the RAPSI process provide?

Simply put, RAPSI is going for perfection, your wholeness. The reason why people don't seem to reach perfection with so many other methods is that they are limited by belief systems – theirs and others'. They don't believe it's possible. We do. We are going for '10'. We want all of us to be 100 per cent integrated and radiating now.

In practice, RAPSI involves exploring, discovering and releasing the structure underpinning our limiting behaviour, including the parts that have been covered over, often with several layers of protection. Beneath this protection, what has invariably been covered is our innermost essence, our light. Enlightenment is not a mystical term, it is literally about releasing and embodying the light, being 'en-light-ened'. It is how we are when we are living fully as human beings in this material world, radiating light, being whole.

The dark spaces in our internal universe may suck in energy from the outer world, including the energy of other people, or we might try to fill the void with distracting or harmful experiences in order to achieve a feeling of aliveness, however simulated and temporary it proves to be. Freeing the light from the inside fills one with the true satisfaction which comes from moving towards wholeness of being. It also frees one from the need to indulge in destructive behaviour. Being able to radiate fully and freely is what we believe we are on earth to achieve. We are here to be the best that we can be, and to contribute fully to the vast tapestry of being. We believe that perfection is both achievable and desirable.

Before you read on, focus on yourself for a moment. Take a deep breath, close your eyes and ask the question: *'On a scale of 1 to 10, where 10 is all of me, how much of me is present here, now, to radiate?'*

Go with the number that pops into your mind.

The Human Story

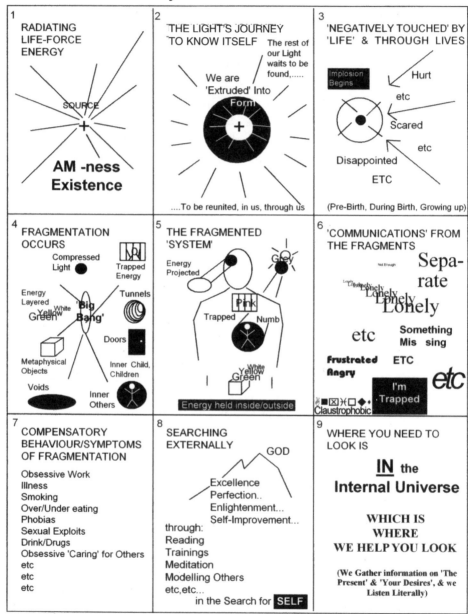

1

RADIATING LIFE-FORCE ENERGY

SOURCE

AM -ness
Existence

2

THE LIGHT'S JOURNEY TO KNOW ITSELF   The rest of our Light waits to be found,.....

We are 'Extruded' Into Form

....To be reunited, in us, through us

3

'NEGATIVELY TOUCHED' BY 'LIFE' & THROUGH LIVES

Implosion Begins

Hurt

etc

Scared

etc

Disappointed

ETC

(Pre-Birth, During Birth, Growing up)

4

FRAGMENTATION OCCURS

Compressed Light

Trapped Energy

Energy Layered
Green   Yellow   White   'Big Bang'

Tunnels

Doors

Metaphysical Objects

Inner Child, Children

Voids

Inner Others

5

THE FRAGMENTED 'SYSTEM'

Energy Projected

Grey

Pink

Trapped   Numb

Yellow
Green   White

Energy held inside/outside

6

'COMMUNICATIONS' FROM THE FRAGMENTS

Not Enough

Sepa-rate

Lonely   Unhappy
Lonely   Lonely
Lonely   Lonely

etc

Something Mis sing

Frustrated   ETC
Angry

I'm ·Trapped

etc

Claustrophobic

7

COMPENSATORY BEHAVIOUR/SYMPTOMS OF FRAGMENTATION

Obsessive Work
Illness
Smoking
Over/Under eating
Phobias
Sexual Exploits
Drink/Drugs
Obsessive 'Caring' for Others
etc
etc
etc

8

SEARCHING EXTERNALLY

GOD

Excellence
Perfection..
Enlightenment...
Self-Improvement...

through:
Reading
Trainings
Meditation
Modelling Others
etc,etc...

in the Search for SELF

9

WHERE YOU NEED TO LOOK IS

IN the
Internal Universe

WHICH IS
WHERE
WE HELP YOU LOOK

(We Gather information on 'The Present' & 'Your Desires', & we Listen Literally)

The Human Story – Part 2

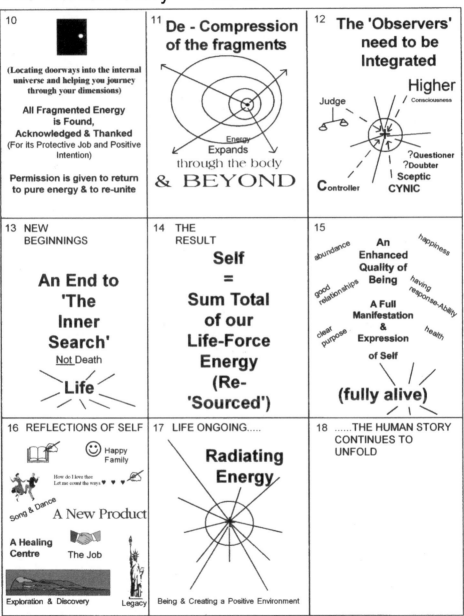

10 (Locating doorways into the internal universe and helping you journey through your dimensions)

All Fragmented Energy is Found, Acknowledged & Thanked (For its Protective Job and Positive Intention)

Permission is given to return to pure energy & to re-unite

11 De - Compression of the fragments

Energy Expands through the body **& BEYOND**

12 The 'Observers' need to be Integrated

Higher Consciousness

Judge

?Questioner
?Doubter
Sceptic
Controller   **CYNIC**

13 NEW BEGINNINGS

An End to 'The Inner Search'
Not Death
Life

14 THE RESULT

Self = Sum Total of our Life-Force Energy (Re-'Sourced')

15 abundance   **An Enhanced Quality of Being**   happiness

good relationships   having response-Ability

A Full Manifestation & Expression of Self

clear purpose   health

(fully alive)

16 REFLECTIONS OF SELF

☺ Happy Family

How do I love thee Let me count the ways ♥ ♥ ♥

Song & Dance   A New Product

A Healing Centre   The Job

Exploration & Discovery   Legacy

17 LIFE ONGOING.....

Radiating Energy

Being & Creating a Positive Environment

18 ......THE HUMAN STORY CONTINUES TO UNFOLD

If it's anything other than 10 – and it's likely to be because you are already engaged in a search for personal development – ask yourself, *'Where's the rest of me?'*

It seems that we are not only releasing energy which has been hidden since we were born, but that the fragmented energy pattern can be, and often is, created before birth, while we are in the womb. Mainstream science is now beginning to confirm energy forms can and do interact with other forms of energy. The foetus responds to energy from its mother, from her body, her thoughts, her emotions and from the world around her. These influences can result in aspects of the energy of the foetus withdrawing, fragmenting and/or going out of body and building up layers of protection even before birth. This is the story told over and over again by people exploring their energetic structure.

After many years of experience helping people to explore their internal universe using the RAPSI process, we believe that our energy, our light* travels through different lifetimes. Whether or not this is 'true' and whether or not you 'believe' it, acting as if it's true allows trapped energy 'from past lives', 'from our ancestral line' or even from other people (alive and dead) to be released and to radiate fully now. There are many case studies in this book where people have spontaneously discovered past lives, so you can judge for yourself whether these are real experiences or whether they are metaphors – and whether it matters.

What matters to us is that the clients achieve wholeness.

*We use the words 'energy', 'light', 'soul', 'spirit' and 'consciousness' interchangeably.

Chapter Two

The RAPSI 5Rs

The basic process of a RAPSI session is the facilitator or therapist asking questions of you, the client, and you giving spontaneous answers – from that part of you that knows. The process as described here is totally oversimplified, but it gives an overview and a structure to the examples throughout the book.

Context

We start by setting a context for the process. Why are you here (in this session/reading this book)? What has prompted you to take the next step on your journey of self discovery? What emotional and physical 'problems' and 'challenges' do you have? What are the major circumstances of your life so far which might be relevant – those that you know about consciously at this stage?*

We also introduce the concept of energy and the fragmented energetic structure which underpins dis-ease and poor performance.

Present State/Desired Outcome

We check with people what their Desired Outcome is, both their life goal and their specific goals for the session/s, and then ask them to assess their Present State – on a scale of 1 to 10 where 10 is their Desired Outcome, how close are they to 10?

There are five main stages to the RAPSI process which we have come to call 'the 5 Rs': Recognition, Relationship, Reconciliation, Release, Radiating. Although this is the basic sequence for the release of each hidden pocket of energy, the process is rarely quite as straightforward. Often more than one part will make itself known during the process,

---

* If you want to answer some of these questions for yourself, go to the Wholeness Programme of exercises which starts on page 143.

which involves back-tracking, and then making sure eventually that all loose ends have been tied up – or, more properly, 'untied'. However the basic sequence is as follows:

Recognition

On the assumption that you, as an energetic structure, are by definition fragmented, the first step is to find the structure. There are lots of ways this structure and its parts make themselves known (see 'Ways In' on page 39). Once located, we enable the parts to become tangible as the client sees them (using inner vision) and acknowledges them. There seems to be a natural sequence here – we start by healing those parts of the structure which present themselves first, and as soon as one part is released, the next will surely make itself known!

Let go of any preconceived notions you have intellectually about the reasons for your current situation. If you could have solved this situation by reason, we assume you would have done it by now. We are working at a different level from reason – although after the experience, your intellect will also be satisfied.

Notice the actual words you use when describing your context, issues and desires. Notice any feelings in your body. Make contact with the words or the feelings by making them tangible – putting one part in one hand and the 'opposing part' on the other (literally, 'on the one hand I feel ... but on the other hand I feel the opposite'). Make the words/feelings visible by discovering their attributes: What colour is it? What might its name be? It may well be coming from an earlier time in your life, so ask it how long it has been there. How old were you when it came into being? How does it feel?

Relationship

As soon as a particular energy fragment becomes tangible, build a relationship with it. Say 'hello'. Always thank it for being there. (All parts of you are there for and with a purpose, doing the best job they can to keep themselves safe ... even if we're going to help them find better ways of doing that.) Ask what its job or function or purpose is. If it doesn't know, ask whether it has a job. What is its positive intention?

How long has it been there? Give it options if it doesn't know or doesn't 'answer' immediately. Since you were an adult or when you were a child? Before or after birth?

Go beyond what you first see. Use x-ray vision to scan, look inside or see through this part, to find anything hidden beyond it. Make a relationship with anything you find. Ask it how it feels about its role. If you get stuck, try taking a bird's eye view to give perspective or short-cut the process. Build relationships with any parts you meet.

Reconciliation

Check whether parts of the structure know about each other. Introduce them to one another. Facilitate negotiations between parts which seem to be in opposition. Ask them whether they know you, who is presumably, but not always, the adult person on the journey. If necessary tell them the date now and update them on your life and desires.

Keep looking through the parts, which are typically layers of protection which you meet one after another. Form a relationship and reconcile each layer with yourself and other layers, until eventually you find source, the pure light, where you need go no further. Have source see the body as its final home and see the rest of the light in the body and bridge the separation between both.

Release

With your intention, help the light shine through, dissolving each layer back into the light as it comes through, integrating it into 'you' so that its energy is fully available to you. As you release light, you may find more parts of the structure, with which you need to build a relationship as before ... until you find the light within them which can also be released.

Radiating

Let the light radiate fully through you, into every cell and fibre of your being – and beyond your skin – so that you are radiating out into the world, fully able to express your true nature in relationship to yourself and others.

If you think this sounds too simple, you're right. People don't usually work this neatly. We are complex energetic systems and we are each unique, having evolved from our unique experiences, often over many lifetimes. This is reflected in the process, where some parts may be released and reintegrated bringing resolution to the stated issue, while other parts make themselves known and lead off in seemingly new directions. Sometimes the process is almost instantaneous. At others there can be a fairly convoluted process of discovering parts within parts, parts blocking the discovery of other parts, parts resisting the process (ie by doing their protective jobs) … as many variations as there are people. Throughout all of this it is the job of the facilitator to keep track of the different levels and layers being explored to make sure they are all given the opportunity to be integrated, as well as to watch and listen closely to aid the exploration of what is not being expressed overtly. The diagram is still oversimplified, but at least it gives the idea that there may be quite a lot of doubling back before a clear sense of resolution is reached.

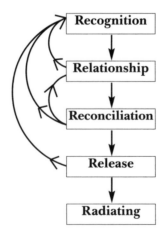

Chapter Three

Sally's story

Sally's story is a detailed case study which shows how the 5R format relates to a RAPSI session with a real client. Many of the later case studies in the book are only given in partial or summary form, but each will have followed a similar sequence of questions and answers. Sally's story, while being unique, as all 'stories' are, is both relatively straightforward and fairly typical of the RAPSI sequence.

Sally's story

This was a demonstration session with Eileen in front of students on a training course. Sally is 38, not married but in a relationship with Phil. In her 20s she experienced ovarian cancer. She had done quite a lot of personal growth work, but had not experienced a RAPSI session before.

Eileen began by chatting to Sally to put her at her ease and giving her an overview of what she might expect from the session (see page 47), telling her to answer questions quickly and instinctively. She also questioned Sally about her Present State and her Desired Outcome. She starts with a 'now score' of 4 out of 10. One of the things Sally says is: *'My mother was very critical. I set high standards.'* Eileen immediately wonders *'Who is 'I'? Where are they speaking from? High up?'* (She got this from the expression 'High standards' – see Literal Listening, page 42.) Also since the mother was critical, there's a good chance that there's a critical part in Sally, possibly an 'inner mother'. Eileen has a starting point. The session proper begins.

E *If there was something critical in you is it masculine or feminine?*

S *Feminine.*

Find location of part inside/outside the body.

E *Is it inside or outside you?*

Something else to find in or above the head?

S *Inside.*

E *Show me.*

S (Shows an area from throat to stomach down the centre)

E *If I could see it?*

S (Sally's head goes back)

E *Does it go all the way up?*

S *I see nothing.*

E *Is it 'light nothing' or 'dark nothing'?*

S *Dark.*

E *What does darkness mean to you? Tell me about darkness.*

S *Darkness to me is not good.*

E *Look up at Darkness and say hello.*

S *OK.*

E *Tell Darkness that it has a job. Am I right?*

S/Darkness *No!*

E *Is darkness doing its job right now?*

S *Yes.*

E *Do I have your permission to talk to Darkness?*

S *Yes.*

E *Do I have your permission, Darkness?*

S/Darkness *Yes.*

E *How long have you been there?*

S/Darkness *A long time.*

E *Your age now, Sally?*

S *38.*

E *How young was she?*

S/Darkness *Two.*

E *Thank you for communicating.*

S/Darkness *OK.*

E *Do you know you have a job?*

S/Darkness *Yes.*

E *Do you enjoy it?*

S/Darkness *Yes.*

E *Is that true?*

S/Darkness *Yes.*

Could be 'nothing' is up? We have learned that 'nothing' is something!

No relationship with 'the dark'.

Step 1 Recognition

It is common to get apparently contradictary answers. The job of Darkness could be to say 'No' or to be critical, so it is doing its job when it says it hasn't got a job.

Get permission from client and 'part' to make direct contact.

Find out location, job, since when, what happened. When did this split occur?

Step 2 Relationship

So-called 'leading questions' can be a quick way of educating the system about itself – and of guiding the client to explore areas which we have noticed or intuited.

E *How is it enjoyable?*

S/Darkness *I'm good at it.*

Mismatch in 'feeling acknowledged' between what the person thinks (Dark is bad) and Darkness's self motivation. No wonder she is in some conflict.

E *Are you rewarded?*

S/Darkness *Yes.*

E *Acknowledged?*

S/Darkness *Yes.*

E *I don't believe you. She thinks you're bad.*

S/Darkness *I'm acknowledged just by doing it.*

E *Are you a good guy or bad guy?*

S/Darkness *A good guy.*

Note the positive intention of being 'critical' – *'I'm taking care of her.'*

E *She doesn't know that. Tell her your job.*

S/Darkness *I'm taking care of her.*

E *Are you surprised, Sally?*

S *No.*

E *You think darkness is bad?*

S *Yes.*

E *You're not surprised?*

S *No.*

E *Are you a fast learner?*

S *Yes.*

Educate the person/their system.

Since this universal pattern of 'light hiding itself' has shown up in all clients, we feel safe in stating that there is 'light at the end of the tunnel', although we ask clients not to believe us until they have experienced it for themselves.

E *Darkness, how specifically do you take care of her?*

S/Darkness *Protection.*

E *I know Darkness wants you to learn. It is about dark spaces in the internal universe. We are all made of energy which becomes fragmented, suppressed. Energy, white light, it's the same. Darkness is simply the most compressed condition of white light energy. If that is true, what would you see when you look into the darkness and through it?*

S *White light.*

E *What can then happen is that the white light comes through the darkness and radiates. Are you willing to look in and see what's there?*

S *Yes.*

E *Tell the darkness that you may be learning it is not a bad guy.*

S *OK.*

E *Take some time to look in and look through, using x-ray vision that you may not know you had. Get curious and find out what's there. Can you thank darkness for doing its job? Only when it feels well thanked, start to look through.*

S *I see another colour around the edges. It's pink.*

E *Everything is 'organic'. Everything is your energy. Always acknowledge everything for the job they may be doing. Say hello to Pink.*

S *OK.*

E *Pink, do you have a job?*

S/Pink *Yes.*

E *Since she was how young?*

S /Pink *Later.*

E *How much later? Three, four, five?*

S/Pink *Ten.*

E *What specifically is your job, Pink?*

S/Pink *A layer.*

E *Part of the layer of protection?*

S/Pink *Yes.*

E *Do you like your job?*

S/Pink *Yes.*

E *What is your job?*

S/Pink *Warmth.*

E *Do you keep something warm?*

S *(Silence)*

E *Pink, say hello to Black. Did you know each other existed?*

S/Pink/Black *Yes.*

E *Are you friendly?*

S/Pink/Black *No.*

E *Pink thank Black, Black thank Pink.*

E *Do you like each other now?*

S/Pink/Black *No.*

E *Black, Pink is part of the protection.*

'X-ray vision' – a process of using 'inner eyes' with outer eyes closed. It differs from visualising or creating an image. It is one of allowing an image to emerge by looking through an energetic layer of colour or an energetic shape.

Questioning the next part/layer to help find the origins of a problem without necessarily needing to get into the content of what happened.

Need to educate Sally/parts that both colours are a layer of protection.

S/Black *Pink is nothing to do with me.*

E *You are both part of the protection. You don't need to believe me.*

Relationship building.

Need for reconciliation.

E emphasises part of the original information she gave Sally: You don't have to 'believe' anything until you have experienced it.

S/Pink/Black *Maybe we can say hello.*

E *Look deeper now, Sally.*

S *There's another colour.*

E *How many colours, I wonder. What colour is it?*

S *Very soft orange.*

E *Do you have a job?*

S/Orange *Yes, working with Pink.*

E *What's your job?*

S/Orange *Something to do with Black.*

E *Part of the protection scheme?*

Taking a bird's eye view is a device for having the person dissociate from what they are 'sensing/ seeing' so as to get another perspective and more information.

S/Orange *Against Black.*

E *Sally, I want you to take the position of a bird and get a bird's eye view. Look beyond Black.*

S *There are two layers more. I see yellow.*

E *What's Yellow's job?*

S *I don't know.*

E *But you do know it's doing a job?*

S *Yes.*

3 Reconciliation

E *Since you were how young?*

S *14.*

E *Protection? Who from?*

S *I don't know.*

E *Protecting something good?*

S *Yes, I think so.*

E *Have Yellow say hello to all the other colours and vice versa.*

S *Yes.*

E *Is there anything beyond Yellow?*

S *It's getting lighter, more like an ivory colour now.*

E *Does Ivory have a job or is it waiting?*

S *It's waiting.*

E *For how long?*

S *For years.*

E *Since how young?*

S *I don't know.*

E *Since two or longer?*

S *Longer.*

E *Before you were born?*

S *After.*

E *One week?*

S *No.*

E *One month?*

S *No. This is wrong. Days.*

E *One, two, three days?*

S *Two days.*

E *Two days in the world and the world sucks?*

S *Yes.*

E *Ivory, what did you do about it?*

S/Ivory *I separated.*

E *You split from your system?*

S/Ivory *Yes.*

E *What have you been waiting for? Her to be wiser, strengthen, to come to get you when the world was a safer place?*

S/Ivory *Yes.*

E *Is this the time?*

S/Ivory *Yes.*

E *Do you know the rest of the system?*

S/Ivory *No.*

E *Do you want to come out?*

S/Ivory *No.*

E *Are you still waiting for things to be better?*

S/Ivory *Safer.*

E *How does it feel being behind Yellow and the colours through to Black?*

S/Ivory *Heavy, tired, nothing.*

E *What do you do with your days? Sleep?*

'Separating' seems to be how the light seeks to protect itself.

She could have waited forever!

The right time to bring energy through is usually 'now', simply because the person finds it.

Life was not safe when the separation happened. We must wake up parts of the person to the reality that it is many years later and that now

22

staying cut-off is not safe for the person.	S/Ivory Yes.
	E *Do you know about the world?*
The Ivory energy has become E's 'client' and she helps it wake up to its condition.	S/Ivory No.
	E *Are you in oblivion?*
	S/Ivory Yes.
Showing the negative consequences of this 'safekeeping': the effects on relationships.	E *Sue, do you have any relationships?*
	S *Yes.*
	E *Who particularly?*
Sally is critical of herself, the first 'relationship'.	S *My partner.*
	E *An intimate relationship?*
	S *Yes.*
	E *On a scale of 1 to 10, how wonderful is your relationship?*
Note the 4 out of 10 measurement again.	S *4 out of 10.*
	E *Your first relationship is with yourself.*
	S *Yes.*
	E *There's a poor relationship between Black and Ivory. You can't win when you play with less than a full deck. 100 per cent fully able to be. What we call radiating. How close to 100 per cent radiating are you?*
	S *40 per cent.*
E educates with humour, and models 'being critical'.	E *That's pretty sad and pathetic?!* (With a twinkle)
	S *It's better than it has been.*
	E *If the situation is not what you want, would you like to go from 40 per cent to 100 per cent?*
	S *Yes.*
	E *If beyond Ivory was the rest of your energy, if when you find the white light, you were to pull it through Ivory, Yellow, Orange, Pink and Black, into Sally, imagine what it would be like. Think what you have been able to achieve with only 40 per cent and what it would be like with 100 per cent. Think about how 'waiting' also means 'weighting', carrying excess weight.*
Weight is one of Sally's issues. Being overweight usually ties in with a part of self 'waiting' which leads to feelings of 'not-enoughness'	*Find the pure white light. You don't need to believe me. If it's there, acknowledge and value it. It's time to go beyond Ivory, look through the layer*

and tell me what you see.

S *There's a lot of Ivory.*

E *Have you thanked Ivory?*

S *No.*

E *Pull back, my apologies. Send appreciation, thanks and gratitude to Ivory and when you have heaped enough thanks on Ivory, look through.*

S *I can see a door.*

E *Thank the door. Everything is energy, your energy. How long have you been there? Since she was how young, Door?*

S/Door *Since zero.*

E *Foetus or before?*

S/Door *(Silence)*

E *(speaks louder) Door, can you hear me?*

S/Door *Just.*

E *Are you far away?*

S/Door *Yes.*

E *Before she was born?*

S/Door *Just.*

E *Open it (the door).*

S *It's small.*

E *Remember this is compressed energy, which can expand.*

S *There's a lock. It looks a bit creepy in there.*

E *If you wanted to keep something safe, you wouldn't put a puppy to guard it.*

S *As I look, it's starting to get darker.*

E *Thank it and begin to welcome the Dark in your universe. Say hello.*

S *Yes.*

E *Dark has had a crappy press agent through history. See the Dark?*

S *It's murky.*

E *Colour?*

S *It's grey brown.*

---

where comfort-eating is a compensatory behaviour. The part never feels 'fed'.

Acknowledgement is the key to moving on.

The next energetic layer, 'a door', shows itself.

Notice that this 'distance' is not imagined, not a metaphor. There is a real experience of distance.

Something scary or creepy is just another layer protecting the light.

We can release the light trapped in the dark (which is itself compressed light). Note that Ivory was light but it hid an even darker layer, so in journeying, one has to keep going.

Humour is allowed – and it helps!

E *Shitty! Say hello. Do you have a job?*

S/Murk Yes.

E *How long?*

S/Murk *Since the beginning.*

E *Is yours a positively intended job, Murk?*

S/Murk *It's the last chance.*

E *Do we look in or down?* (Sally's head is down)

S/Murk *Down.*

Uses nickname to lighten the experience.

E *Are you excited Murk/Smirk?* (Murk often leads to water or brown earth.)

This was a learning point for the students. Looking for 'light' and 'healing' in the west often involves looking up. It's easy to forget the energies trapped below us and below in us. Note the 'coldness/frozenness'. We wonder about the cause of her ovarian cancer (note her hand on abdomen).

S *It's getting cold.* (Puts hand on abdomen)

E *Look down quickly.*

S *There's something in cold storage.*

E *Look beyond.*

S *It's getting lighter.*

E *Say hello. I'm looking for source down here.*

S *OK, it's definitely getting lighter.*

E *Keep looking down.*

S *It's getting warmer. I can see the door again.*

E *Are you looking from the other side?*

S *No.*

E *Is it another door?*

S (Silence)

E *Say hello. How long have you been here?*

S *It's bigger.*

E *It's time to open you now, is there a lock?*

S *There's a window.*

E *See who or what's in there.*

S *Nothing.*

E *Light nothing or dark nothing?*

S *Light.*

E *Dissolve the door.*

S *It's coming.*

E *Do you know the way back?*

S *No.*

E *Find the light?*

S *Yes.*

E *Have it come and dissolve the Murk.*

S *It's doing it.*

E *Have it thank and dissolve the little door – Ivory – Yellow – Orange – Pink – Black.*

S *There's a hole, it's pouring through, and it's dissolving the other way. I feel peculiar.*

E *This will affect your neurology, I will not let you go till you tell me you feel fine. Presumably there is light now in your physical body?*

S *Yes.*

E *Is it consolidating or expanding?*

S *Consolidating.* (Shows chest/throat)

E *The light needs to expand fully into all you, right to cellular level.*

S *OK.*

E *Now you need to learn that the light does not need to stop at the skin line but can radiate out to reach, for example, to where Phil is.*

S *I am having some difficulty, it's as if there's a boundary, a glass wall around me.*

E *Do you think it is a good idea now to radiate beyond that wall?*

S *Yes.*

E *Congratulate the Wall. How long has it been there?*

S/Wall *Since the beginning.*

E *Imagine Phil trying to be with someone who is living in a glass bowl which he cannot get beyond.*

S *He doesn't know it consciously.*

E *If you free you, you free him also.*

S *It has begun to crack, shatter.*

E *You know that you have found your warmth. Intentionally have your energy begin to radiate out.*

S *It's changing.* (She relaxes markedly)

Step 4 Release

Things begin to happen almost faster than the questions can be asked. Is 'peculiar' a new feeling or is something not right?

Step 5 Radiating

Consolidating is what people do typically. They need to learn to have their energies expand and radiate.

The wall or shield keeps people out and self in/safe, but a major part of self is outside our own wall, and behind the wall we feel 'trapped' or unsafe. The wall is also our energy and it takes energy to maintain it.

	E *Is it melting?*
Coldness – still something to complete.	S *I can feel the coldness.* (Looks down)
	E *Is it down?*
We have to learn that every scrap of energy in form, wherever it is, is usually ours and needs to be recycled back into us to then expand and radiate out.	S *It's now stuff on the floor, gooey.*
	E *Everything is energy, light, and has a use – even 'gooey'. Invite the energy to come into you.*
	S *It's done.*
	E *Did you know that you were a healer?*
	S *No.*
An empowering statement – we make them any chance we get.	E *Have all the light expand through you bringing warmth.*
	S *Yes.*
	E *Now that you are radiating from inside you, you can bring down, up, in, all the rest of your light to add to the radiance. How much of you is now here, able to be with Phil? You were at 4 out of 10.*
So 30 per cent more of Sally is in the present in a session lasting just less than an hour.	S *7 out of 10.*
	E *How do you feel?*
	S *Able to be a fuller expression of me.*

Typically we ask how the person feels three or four times as the integration process unconsciously continues, and to check that the person is in a positive place and can leave. We also want to gather positive feedback and bring this into the person's awareness – which can also give markers about work in a future session.

We noted Sally's next step as working on something on the top of her head, in her right brain and in the back of the neck (places that she marked out with her gestures during the session and from sympathetic feelings that we experienced). We will check that out next time.

Chapter Four

Where are you now?

At the beginning of any exploratory session there are certain things which need to be clarified. Firstly we want to find out more about the client. Then we have to agree the ground rules for the session/s and give the client information about what to expect.

The starting point for any self exploration is to take stock of your current situation: *What are you doing currently? What's important about doing this? How well is your life working now? What do you want?*

The reasons people start working with us are many and varied. Sometimes they know that they have specific mental, emotional or physical problems. More often, they just feel that there is something not quite right or that there must be something more to life. There have even been some people who have already done a lot of self-development work who want to move towards perfection in their lives, or to get to that one stuck spot they haven't been able to shift yet. Others are just curious. Are any of the following reasons people have given for starting this work also true for you?

- *I don't feel good, positive, healthy, 'right'.*
- *I lack energy, vision, positivity, a good decision-making strategy.*
- *I keep getting myself into trouble.*
- *I attract the wrong people, relationships.*
- *I am disappointed in life, in myself.*
- *I had expectations about my life that I simply couldn't achieve.*
- *I have habits and behaviours that I want to change.*
- *I blame others, but I know it really comes back to me.*
- *I seem to be successful but I just feel there should be more.*
- *My life is pretty wonderful. Now I'm going for perfection.*

We always give clients a questionnaire to complete either before or during the initial session which establishes some of the background and other information about their lives – significant illnesses or events from their past, current problems, etc, as well as what they want – but the relevant issues also come out during the exploratory sessions.

Right from the beginning, as the client and the facilitator chat and begin to get comfortable with one another, the facilitator is watching the client and listening to the language they use, looking for hints as to where fragments of energy might be hidden (see 'Ways in', page 35).

Present State

Our first goal is to establish clearly the person's 'Present State', so we may ask: *How well is your life working now? What problems and challenges are you experiencing? On a scale of 1 to 10, where 10 is what you want, how close to 10 are you?*

It's interesting how people seem to know the answer to this last question, even though realistically it is so imprecise. The trick is to go with the figure that seems to come to you, rather than trying to work it out logically. But having come up with a figure, say 5 out of 10, the really interesting question is, what's stopping you from being at 10? Where is the rest of you, the remaining 50 per cent? The answer is that the missing pieces are energy, or light, which has hidden itself under layers of protection (also made of energy or light), with the result that it is not currently available to you. It is the job of the RAPSI process to help you discover and release this light and integrate it into your system so that you can operate with all your resources available to you.

We then ask people to be more precise, and give a figure on the 1 to 10 scale for the various aspects of their lives. We ask them to evaluate how satisfied they are with their relationship with themselves, their partner, their children, other members of their family, friends, colleagues, with their health, their work, their finances, their living environment and their leisure time. In addition we ask them to put a figure on their clarity of purpose and their sense of well-being. We might then ask for some clarification of any particularly low scores, as a way of finding the areas in which they are looking for improvement.

We also establish the person's bottom line Desired Outcome (see next chapter), so by now we have enough information to get on with the session straightaway, but for the sake of clarity for people doing this work alone, there is more work that can be done to establish the Present State. Here are some of the questions you can ask yourself:

Challenges

What problems, challenges or issues do I face? List them. Examples of the sorts of things people have said at this point are:

- *I have crap relationships. Each woman I meet finds me attractive, cute on the outside and we have a good time, but when I get a few months into the relationship, I feel as if part of me has pulled away, as if I was never involved or committed, and the relationship ends.*
- *No money. Whenever money comes to me, I lose it, waste it. It's as if I want to stay poor, feel safer, stay small.*
- *Ill health. My ankles swell up, I have a tight throat, my breathing is shallow, I get kidney stones, easily feel very tired, no energy. I suffer from depression.*
- *I am not getting the best out of myself, not reaching my potential. I sit in meetings watching what is going on; I don't feel part of things. I feel shy and anxious, my heart pumps very fast.*

Similarly you can look for more precise evidence of problems in your life. The sorts of questions which might prompt this are:

- *Where have I compromised myself in my life?*
- *What secrets do I keep? Which bits do I keep hidden?*
- *If my life ended right now what regrets would I have?*
- *What do I complain about?*
- *Who do I blame and for what?*
- *What habits do I have that I would like to change?*
- *What obsessions do I have? Food, alcohol, drugs, shopping, sex, work, caring for others...?*
- *Am I accident prone? In what way?*
- *Am I a victim? In what way?*
- *How do I limit myself?*
- *How is my health? When in my life has it not been good?*
- *Who do I most take after – parents, grandparents, who? What do I like, dislike about the similarities?*
- *What would make life better?*
- *What would make life perfect?*

CNDs

At some point in your journey, it will be important to establish any underlying recurring negative feelings or emotions you have (fear, anger, sadness, etc). We call these your 'CNDs', your Chronic Negative Deposits. They are useful later for identifying your 'Unconscious Equation' (see page 55), and in the meantime they might indicate areas for exploration.

I/Self relationship

Another important question which is key to your getting to '10', or wholeness of being, is your relationship with yourself. Have you ever said something along the lines of 'on the one hand I'm like this, but on the other hand I'm somebody completely different'? Have there been times when you've wanted two contradictory things? Do you feel parts of you tugging in different directions?

If your energy is fragmented, then there are going to be parts (energetic fragments) hidden in many different places, but what seems to be universal is that we have two distinct parts of ourselves which identify themselves as being 'us'. We call them 'I' and 'Self' (or 'I' and 'Me'). People's first relationship is with themselves. In some cases this means that the two different parts, I and Self, have a relationship with each other, which may be good or bad. Sometimes there is no such relationship and I and Self may not even know of each other's existence. How you relate to yourself usually affects how you relate to everybody else, particularly your partner. Conversely, when there are chronic problems in your relationships with other people, it can be an indication that you need to work on your relationship with yourself for starters (and then on becoming whole). Once that's reconciled, other relationships seem to run much more smoothly.

So what is your relationship with yourself? The starting point is simply to think about the question, and then ask yourself what others would say about you in answer to the question. Take it further. Describe your relationship with yourself by filling in the blank in the sentence: *I .... myself*, for example:

- *I love myself.*
- *I feel sorry for myself.*
- *I blame myself.*
- *I judge myself.*
- *I criticize myself.*

- *I hate myself.*
- *I am disappointed in myself.*
- *I push myself.*
- *I hold myself back.*
- *I condemn myself.*

Having identified your current relationship with yourself, you can use the RAPSI process to reconcile any parts which are not currently working well together. Before getting on to that, however, it is important to know what it is you want to achieve from your session.

Chapter Five

Your Desired Outcome

What do you want from this session, for your life? What is your Desired Outcome? What are all your Desired Outcomes?

Strangely enough it isn't always easy to answer this question. Most people know what they don't want, or what they want to get away from, but surprisingly few have a clear idea of what they do want in this life. Why not think about it now? By all means start by listing the things you don't want, the things that need to change, but then look through the list and see what it is that would replace each of these negative aspects of your life. Look at everything. Go for perfection. You're not going to get it unless you know what 'it' is, and if you believe that change is possible, then you might as well go for the best that life can possibly be. Describe your perfect life. What will it look like, sound like, feel like? Where will you be living? Who with? What will you be doing each day, each month, each year?

Spend a few moments thinking about any negative consequences of this new and perfect life. Who will your friends be? Is this a long-term sustainable way of living, or have you just described a holiday period away from your real life? Make sure that this is really what you want for your everyday life.

Think about some of the 'bigger' questions too. What do you sense is your major purpose in this lifetime? Do you have any 'minor' purposes, things you want to achieve along the way? What sort of person are you deep down? What sort of person do you want to be? How will others describe you? What will they notice about you?

Our definition of perfection, what we call 'authentic excellence', is the experience of being fully who you were meant to be, feeling complete, fully expressive and freely radiating your energy into the world, free from blocks, inner conflicts, withholdings, inauthentic behaviour and dis-ease. How near are you to being authentically excellent? What could bring you closer?

The bottom line

Read what you have written as your Desired Outcome(s) and ask yourself, 'If I had all of that, what would that give me?' If, for example, you wrote that you want a big house, a happy and loving relationship, a sizeable retirement fund and that you will be contributing to your community, it might give you the chance to slow down.

Given that answer, ask yourself again, 'And what would that give me?'

In our example, it might give you the chance to relax.

Continue with this process until you get to what feels like your 'bottom line' answer – which will be expressed as how you want to feel. With your big house and the opportunity to relax, you might feel comfortable. And with that you might feel peaceful, warm and alive.

Finally ask yourself, 'Is there any other feeling or experience I want to add?' How about joy? Anything else?

It is important that your actual bottom line Desired Outcome is described as a way of being and feeling, which is what will fuel the doing, achieving and having.

There is a checking process to make sure that your Desired Outcome really is all you desire. It involves visualising and questioning your Future Self who has achieved your Desired Outcome and is living in your ideal future. How would that person cope with the life you are living now and any issues from your past? What would be different? What advice do they have for you? How close are you to being that Future Self? What would you lose by becoming your ideal future self?

This last question is an important one. Even if your immediate response is that you would lose nothing, it is worth probing further to try to bring to the surface any unconscious fears. Will you still be recognisable as you? Will your friends and family still like you? Will you want or be able to make new friends? Are you being unrealistic? Is the vision too grand for the you you know yourself to be?

But having played devil's advocate, look again at what you will gain from achieving this ideal future.

The RAPSI process is about helping you achieve your bottom line Desired Outcome. And even if life has been a struggle until now and may continue to be a struggle for others, we believe that life can truly be as wonderful as you want it to be.

And when you become authentically excellent and reach perfection, do you stop? (As one client asked, do you die?) No. Clients who achieve their '10' do not stop learning, expanding and growing. On the contrary, they now have all the resources they need to live fully in the world and learn positively rather than through a series of accidents and mishaps. You too can reach your '10'.

While you are on your RAPSI journey, your Desired Outcome may magnify as you discover what's possible.

So far this chapter has been about a conscious process and you might have done something similar with other self-help facilitators. It will certainly be familiar to anyone who has done NLP. It is therefore now important to let clients know what to expect from a RAPSI session, particularly where things might be different from what they have experienced before.

The first question we are often asked is, is perfection possible? Can I really reach my Desired Outcome, my authentic excellence?

The answer is yes. Perfection is possible, achievable and desirable, and the process can be very fast. People are freed from their misery quickly. Having said that, some clients have more to clear than others, and some need support over a longer period. So 'swift' is not always the goal. Long-lasting success is. But part of the RAPSI process is to educate the client to understand both what we mean by the word 'perfection' and that it is achievable.

For many, perfection by definition is some unattainable state which involves removing oneself from the world and living in some kind of 'heaven'. As one woman said at the end of a talk Eileen was giving, *'Who wants peace anyway?'* Frankly, we agree. Peace can sound pretty boring if your idea of it is to sit around doing nothing. It certainly isn't what we are working towards.

Similarly someone who felt he had reached his '10' was worried about feeling open and vulnerable. If he walked down Oxford Street, wouldn't he be open to all the negative influences of anyone he walked past? Wouldn't he have lost all his protection?

On the spur of the moment, Eileen invited him create in his mind's eye five metaphysical shit-balls out of the worst things he could imagine. (It was all that came to mind at the time!) She held them for him, and then in quick succession she threw them at him one by one. First of all he looked amazed, and then a huge grin came over his face. When he was asked what had happened, he said that they had all either burst into light on contact with him, gone right through him and burst into light, or just burst into light as they left her hand.

However, even when people are confident that they want to strive for excellence, there is some confusion about the definition of the word. For many it is synonymous with 'performance excellence' and involves success in the material world or the need to achieve. But many people who seem from the outside to be successful are actually in conflict inside. How often do we hear of 'successful' people with all the trappings of material success who suddenly have a 'mid-life crisis'? They strive for years to reach 'the top' and when they get there it doesn't bring the expected sense of fulfilment they were wanting.

We define perfection as 'Authentic Excellence'. This is the excellence which comes from within, from feeling complete and whole, regardless of where you are or who you are with. It is a the full experience of being, rather than doing or having. It means that you feel excellent whatever you are doing here in the real world and feel fully engaged, fully passionate and able to feel appropriately to a situation. It is a way of engaging with the world completely. What some have described as 'being fully present'.

In our terms it involves being totally whole, fully radiating, having discovered, released and embodied all aspects of your energetic being.

Nor is this perfection to be forever a future goal. In fact it is an important part of the RAPSI process to make contact with your Future Self (which may be your age or younger or older than you), since this too is part of your energy which is being held at a distance. We ask clients to visualise Future Self and build a relationship with it. Ask it how it has felt to be the 'front runner'. It may well have been feeling lonely and exposed, having to do all the hard work and dragging you along behind. Alternatively it might feel detached and apparently fabulous, satisfied and complete – all the things you want to feel. Either way, the energy of Future Self needs to come home into the present you in now-time.

Simply engaging in this exploration can begin the process of bringing the energy of Future Self into you, but for a more tangible merging of energy, it could be as simple as them walking into you bringing the resources you need to help you create your ideal future now. Or you might need to see the light in them, have them see the rest of the light in you – and possibly in parts of your energy beyond you. (There is typically a book-end effect where a pocket of energy above, in front, to the right, or wherever, has a corresponding pocket of energy below, behind, to the left, etc.) You then help all those energies to merge in your body, and then to radiate beyond.

There are various points we would like to highlight:

- We can project energy into our future.
- Sometimes Future Self thinks that it has the body. It may be unaware that the Present Self exists, let alone that it would be desirable for you to merge your energies.
- Having a Future Self out there acts as a beacon that we move towards, or it may be a 'pathfinder' out in front, or a protective shield or the image you'd like to present to the world.
- Having a Future Self can give the feeling of always running to catch up: *'I start things well but I have difficulty completing them.' 'I think it will be OK when I reach x or achieve y, but it still does not feel satisfying enough when I get there.'* Until Future Self merges with you, it will always be ahead. You will never get there.
- When you reach a goal, Future Self will have moved on so Present Self feels pressured to keep going, unable to fully appreciate achievements.
- The biggest learning is that the energy of Future Self belongs in the body of Present Self, in present time. Without it, at best there will be struggle, at worst, the future will never be realised.

37

We realise that this may go against some of the self development techniques you may already have learnt. We'd rather you think of it as the next step.

If you have done NLP work and have been in the habit of maintaining a 'time line' with a future and a past which you visit to help with self development, we want to help you to collapse it now and bring all of your resources into the present. Or if you hold a 'possibility', a word or vision to help you be effective and move forwards, we advocate bringing those energies into the present.

All the while you leave your resources in another place, whether it be the future or the past, they are not immediately available to you. You have to 'visit' or 'summon' them every time you need to use their energy. With RAPSI, the goal is that all of your resources are available at all times. You no longer have pieces of energy held separately. You are whole.

Yes but ... *isn't this just NLP?*

The concepts of Present State and Desired State (which we call Desired Outcomes) come originally from Neuro-Linguistic Programming, as does the notion of working with fragmented parts of the person's internal universe. However, the RAPSI concept of the energetic structure is multi-dimensional. RAPSI is always working to incorporate the light of wholeness, of being, including any observers, and integrating the energy into the present, allowing the light of everything, incluhding source, to radiate and permeate every aspect of you and your life. RAPSI is working towards Authentic Excellence – our idea of perfection.

Chapter Six

Ways in

Once someone has decided to come for a RAPSI session, how do we find the ways in to discover trapped energy? We look and listen for signs of their energetic structure and 'doorways' into this system, which can manifest themselves in many different ways. All the clients need to do is to begin describing why they have come and the doorways become obvious. These are then made tangible by acknowledging them, and the process has started.

We know that energy hides itself behind layers of protection (which are also energy taking different forms), but we also know that trapped energy wants to be found and released, so it sends out signals. These signals can be in the form of emotional or mental unease or distress, or physical illness or disease (literally dis-ease). If someone comes with a 'vague feeling' of unease, we might simply ask where they notice the 'vague feeling' or have that feeling name itself and ask it questions (what its job is, how long it's been there, etc). With a physical illness, the site of the illness becomes the doorway. *'Thank the pain in your knee for communicating itself. What in your knee is feeling in pain?'* Classic physical doorways are tension, especially of a chronic nature, headaches, migraine, etc, pain from physical symptoms, illness, skin problems, tumours, poor hearing or eyesight ('I-sight'), heart and kidney problems, infection, even sprained muscles or broken bones. Any and all of these might be a signal that something is held or missing and that there is energy to be found. They can all be used as doorways to find the first layer of protection.

People also indicate doorways with their gestures and non-conscious movements. If someone keeps gesturing off to the right as they speak, we might have them look for energy outside them and to their right, if they tap themselves on the chest, then it is likely that there is some trapped energy in their chest. If they have difficulty seeing into an area, we may help them describe a doorway: *'I notice you're gesturing a lot towards your left temple. Look into your left temple. If there was a door*

Classic physical doorways in terms used by clients

- Head
- Left and right temples
- Middle of forehead, Third Eye (centre of forehead, forward projections
- Through the eyes
- Within or at the back of the left and right brains and projections outwards
- Centre of head (behind the third eye)
- Various places on top of and above the head
- At the top of the spine, by the brainstem
- Ears
- Throat
- Front, middle, back, upper chest
- In and behind heart
- Lungs, diaphragm
- Between the shoulder blades
- Arms and hands

- Solar plexus
- Stomach, upper stomach
- Liver, gall bladder, spleen, bowels, kidneys, bladder, intestinal tract,
- Lower abdomen, pelvis
- Anus and below
- Sexual organs, womb, ovaries
- Legs, knees, feet, below the feet
- Around the body
- Out left and out right in the future
- Out in front of the body as walls and shields with a self beyond, or a self striding into the future with its back turned to the present, etc
- Behind the body as a presence, a pusher or a brake on the system
- Above the body and way up into the cosmos; way down into the earth's core and beyond
- … and more!

there, a door to something that has been signalling its presence, what would it look like? Can you describe it? How big is it? What shape is it? Does it have a colour?' Or we might simply have them look 'in that direction' with their inner eyes open to see what they see.

Body scanning and energy mapping

One key way to help people find their own doorways is the process of 'body scanning' and 'energy mapping'. For this you use your inner eyes and see or sense/see areas of colour or energy within the body. It can be helpful with this exercise to draw in the coloured areas on outline drawings representing your body. (See colour pictures or try it for yourself with Exercise 13 on page 158.)

People draw their energetic system in whichever way seems or feels right to them and the maps can take many forms, with energy appearing in or outside the body, as isolated parts or complete bands or swathes of energy. Sometimes they can give names to each part or each colour, such as 'muddle, scared and succeeding', 'barrier', 'frame', 'pain', 'out of focus', 'anger', sad and lonely', etc. The energy map seems to be our telepathic understanding of our energy system made tangible.

Having drawn whichever views are necessary to show all the energy they can sense in their system (the recognition stage), the person is asked to thank each colour (which becomes a doorway) for its positively intended job (of protection). The colours are also introduced to one another and asked to talk to one another – frequently they do not know of one another's existence and that in their own ways they have all been doing a similar job of protection. The areas have also probably never been acknowledged or thanked before and this important stage begins the client's relationship with them and their relationship wth one another, which in turn begins the process of reconnecting the isolated parts, helping them move towards wholeness. We can then start the process of questioning to find out specifics and move into the process.

As we work, we also tune in to our clients. We can sense in our bodies when we are feeling a client's symptoms (eg a tense spot) – and this may even start before the session when we're preparing our notes for the session. If you've never tried it, then an easy starting point is to match their body posture, body tone, stance, head position, breathing rate, etc. Then relax, suspend disbelief, and just 'tune in'. (With practice this all becomes second nature and you just 'tune in'.) The result is that we usually feel the physical symptoms that the client is experiencing – which certainly makes asking questions easier, as we have a pretty good idea where we're going. The only proviso is that we check out any assumptions we make.

Once the client has identified a doorway, we ask them to look into the place and say what they see. They may answer with a colour (eg *Yellow, Grey Cloud, Black*) or some inner form. Whatever it is, they are asked to acknowledge its presence, address it by name (*'Hello, Yellow'*) and thank it for being there and for doing its job or function which they are learning is positively intentioned. This process helps to bring the energy more clearly into view and become more tangible. The client can then start a dialogue to discover what that job or function is, how long it's been doing it, how old they were when it was created, etc, before looking inside or through that doorway to find the next layer. When they find that layer, they find that it too is a doorway, and then within or through that, the next energetic layer of protection is another doorway. When the layer takes the form of a person, they may find that the doorway into them is in the same position as the one they originally identified in themselves, which is an indicatation that the inner energetic form is crafted from their energy and is displaying the same symptoms as them. When they find an inner person, eg a mother, or a younger self, the layers within them may also take the form of colours, shapes or 'inner others' (other people, or younger selves). We call these layers within layers 'nested energies'. It is assumed that everything is made out of the client's own energy unless we find out differently.

Literal Listening

A major way of locating doorways is by 'listening literally'. With your body as the centre point, you can start to locate the fragments of yourself and place where they are, aided by the language that you use. If somebody says they are 'depressed' or 'suppressed', we know that something spacially 'down' in their body or below their feet needs to be found. An expression such as *'I left it behind'* might get us looking behind them, probably to the left.

Our language is full of metaphors – not in the literary meaning, but where one thing stands for another. Advertisers often talk in the language of war as they 'launch a campaign', 'set targets', 'aim high' and 'attack problems'. We might use the language of gardening to talk about 'planting' and 'nurturing' 'the seed' of an idea, etc. But in RAPSI we do not think these metaphors are chosen randomly. These are parts of our non-conscious mind expressing itself and its reality literally. If you say you *'feel the weight of the world on your shoulders'*, you are likely to be sagging and feeling constantly weighed down. What we do is listen to the language a person uses and picture it literally, as it is invariably a key to their energetic structure.

When listening literally, we also listen for alternative spellings of a word. Problems with your 'eye' might actually be related to a part of

---

Read through the list below.
Identify where you would look for hidden energy.
What questions would you want answers to if you were looking for hidden energy?

- I'm always running to catch up
- I push myself
- I hold myself back
- I maintain an image
- I shield myself
- I feel downright unhappy
- I feel down
- I am hard on myself
- left behind
- I'm always left out
- right on
- great weight/wait on my shoulders
- haven't a leg to stand on
- pain in the bum/neck
- right in front of my eyes
- in your face
- looking forward to ...
- off the top of my head
- I'm all over the place

- keep on your toes
- on the one hand/other hand
- beside myself
- it's all over my head/above me
- below the belt
- heartache/heartfelt
- on the tip of my tongue
- at my fingertips
- up in the air
- stabbed in the back
- fell into my lap
- on my knees
- over and above
- it's beyond me
- everything's up in the air
- they're always under my feet
- stand up for myself
- I'm my own worst enemy
- deep down

---

your identity – 'I'. Often the word 'weight' can be understood as 'wait' (or vice versa) – the long wait of a piece of energy wanting to be released. Weight problems can frequently be resolved with RAPSI.

We are curious when clients say something like *'I am running to keep up'* or *'I push myself'*, as to where they are speaking from. Who is 'I' and who is 'myself'? *'Where is that part speaking from? Is it inside you or outside your body?'* We ask them to answer quickly and intuitively so that they don't logic this to death. They answer 'inside me'. We ask, *'Inside, neck up or neck down?'* They answer 'neck up' (feeling that it comes from their neck or head). *'Where neck up?'* (We can choose to be more precise about the locations front, back, left, right, centre, etc, as we have been watching where they have been unconsciously pointing.) They answer 'my left temple' and we use that as a doorway for them to look into to find the 'I' that feels it is running to catch up (we need to find out 'catch up to whom and where'), or is feeling pushed (and 'who is doing the pushing and from where?').

Literal Listening, then, is the skill, as a facilitator, to build three-dimensional pictures from the words spoken, gradually adding pieces of the three-dimensional/multi-dimensional puzzle, and keeping track of the pieces, perhaps by drawing a picture to mark them out. We know that there are 'book-ends' in this energetic structure. So, if you said I am running to catch up, there is likely to be something out in front of the body and something behind. Likewise, if there's left, there's right, if there's something up, there's something down, within or below the body. What does running to catch up feel like? What if they never do? Have they ever caught up, how does that feel? You can see how the questions that we ask partially come from using language to make pictures and then using the pictures to be curious and gather more information.

Now that you are aware of this skill, why not watch someone being interviewed on television and listen to their language. Notice the idioms they use, particularly those which describe directions or locations. Or read an article or an autobiography and notice the language that the person uses and wonder about their energetic structure. Breakfast with your family will never be the same again!

Other doorways

During our sessions with clients, we can also often notice when people are hearing inner voices, or voices which seem to come from around them. They typically put their head on one side, look from side to side or touch their ear/s. They may also say things such as '*I say to myself ...*', '*Something tells me ...*'. Talking directly to these voices can lead to the beginning of some fruitful information gathering and the start of some journeying.

As well as watching and listening closely, we also energetically match our clients (this has now become an unconscious process) to feel places in our bodies which give us indications of their experience. It can guide us to ask the right questions to help us shortcut the questioning process. When clients free a blocked piece of energy, we may feel the same tingling, energy buzz, their ability to breathe more deeply, a sense of relaxation, etc, or where a sensation of blockage remains, to suspect that something is hidden, not yet located or is being unsaid, which we can then verify. It's another way of helping us to monitor progress.

There are, too, other types of doorways that we look/feel out for. As well as physical feelings, people might sense the presence of another energy – someone standing behind them, a feeling of being watched, an awareness of something which doesn't seem to originate with them (which may manifest as a spirit attachment), or a past or future self. We may sense these types of feelings too.

There are many starting points for discovering and

> Any of the following are indications of the energetic structure letting you know that there is trapped energy to be discovered:
> - Physical doorways, indicated by pain, discomfort, gestures
> - Emotional feelings located physically in the body
> - Disease, illness, injury, pain
> - Literal language
> - Inner exploration, possibly aided by body scanning and energy mapping
> - Inner or outer voices which may or may not seem to belong to the client
> - Sensed other presences

exploring the magnificent energetic structure and finding trapped energy. Remember, the energy wants and needs to be found and is continuously sending out messages, purposefully or not, and clues as to its whereabouts. It is up to us, as facilitators and/or as seekers after wholeness, to listen to and act on those messages by becoming curious, taking this level of existence seriously and beginning to explore.

Chapter Seven

A RAPSI session

We've established a rapport between facilitator and client. We've discovered the client's Present State and bottom line Desired Outcome. The client has an idea of what's about to happen and we've noticed, through literal listening and watching the client's gestures, some possible ways of starting. What happens next?

When we (Eileen and Clive) are working with a client, we will be asking questions (and the questions we ask are one of the most important aspects of the process), giving information, and energetically matching them so that we can usually feel how they're feeling and where there's still work to be done. However, we're writing this chapter in the form of instructions to you for working alone.

Exploring your internal universe

This is a relatively straightforward journey (insofar as any inner journey is straightforward) to help you begin exploring your inner universe. Your starting point is to produce an energy map by body scanning (see page 40). Before you start, ask yourself, on a scale of 1 to 10, how much of you is fully present now. When you get your answer, wonder about the rest.

Recognition Choose a doorway. The first step is your 'recognition' of the start point, and then, a step at a time, seeing through the layers of protection to find and release the light. Remember that the start point might be a voice, a colour, a shape, a form, apparently solid objects, mist, a human being (known to you or not, alive or dead, possible a younger or future you), a spirit, a presence, an alien, a tunnel, void, 'nothingness', a dark space, a 'black hole', shining energy ... the list is endless. But all these things are energy and part of your energetic structure. All are positively intentioned. For simplicity, we're going to use the word 'part' or 'layer' whatever form it takes, and for this example we're going to start with a colour.

Relationship Make contact with the colour. Say 'hello'. Thank it for doing its job. Ask what its job is. Ask it if it knows that its most important job is protecting the source of light, yet to be discovered. Thank it for whatever response you get. You are now building a relationship with the part. Make sure you let your system know that it doesn't have to believe anything you say unless and until it gets its own internal confirmation. Suggest it simply acts 'as if' what you say is true in order to find out.

Recognition/Relationship After talking to the part, look through it and see what lies beyond this top layer. It may be a colour, an image, yourself as a younger person – or pretty much anything you can imagine. Whatever you get, acknowledge it, thank it for doing its job and ask what its job is. Give it permission to communicate telepathically with you. You might also ask how long it has been there, whether it is pleased to be found and whether it knew it was going to be found today. You need to recognise and build a relationship with each part/layer you meet, including the light at source when you meet it. Ask how they feel? Are they happy, or are they lonely? How do they feel about doing their job? Would they like a rest?

Reconciliation As you meet each part, ask it if it knows how old you are now and what the date is now. (Trapped energy often doesn't realise that the world has moved on.) If necessary, tell it about your life today. Introduce parts to other parts. Ask if they knew each other existed. Explain to them that they are part of the same energetic system, all helping to protect a dimension of pure source light. Ask each part whether it would like to be reunited into the you of today. (If it says no, respect that for now and retire, or move on to another part, but in our experience it will say yes.) Ask if it knew it was going to be found today. (It may well say yes. The reason you are doing this work is because some part of you knows that light needs to be released. The 'right time' to do this work is the time you do it.)

Ask the part what it will gain from being united with you (often the chance to have a rest and to live fully). Ask it what it will bring the you of today. (It will probably bring you the positive quality of the job it has been doing, so that this quality will be available to you in your

48

everyday life, rather than being trapped in a part of you that you cannot easily access.)

Release Some parts may feel that they can just re-integrate into you with all their energy. Others may need to be dissolved into light so their energy can be absorbed into the you of today. Some just need to be found and released. The system will know what to do. It will be the right thing for you. The finding, recognition and relationship can start the release. Thank it for the job it has been doing all this time, tell it that you'll be fine as soon as it becomes a fully-integrated part of you and that it has total permission to be released from its job.

The energy in the form of a part may well know how to integrate with you and the release may move very swiftly. An outer light tells you, for example, that the re-entry point is through the top of your head and you watch it and then feel it come in. Or it may be a younger you that expands from your stomach or walks in from the back and expands all through you. Trust that it will know how to do that – and it will. Welcome it into you and feel its presence.

Continue looking through each layer, repeating this process of acknowledgement, questioning, forming relationships and fostering reconciliation until you discover the white light. Talk to the light as you would to any other part. Acknowledge it and thank it for being there. Check that it really is the white light. Ask if there's anything beyond. (Some layers can be very similar to white light, while still being protective layers.) Sometimes the white light of source is preceded by black, or something you particularly don't like or find scary. Don't worry. It's just another layer doing a good job of protecting the light and you. It will dissolve, just as other parts dissolve.

Ask whether the light is ready to be released and to bring its energy into the you of today. If it says no, thank it. It may simply still be doing its job, which could be 'to say no'. It could mean that you have not understood or acknowledged it enough, or you have not done enough to inform it of the positive benefit to you, or there may be another part of you holding it in place which you need to negotiate with first. If it persists in saying no, then you may have to resolve your Unconscious

Equation first – see Chapter Eight – as there may be some compelling positive intentions for holding on to a pattern of behaviour that results in negative consequences which would be released with the light. You might ask what would enable it to say yes and be released.

When the light says yes, have it look through all the layers of protection you have journeyed through to find it until it finds the part of the light which is already radiating in the you of today. Ask the two sources of light to make contact and say hellos. Encourage mutual appreciation.

Then, with your intention, help to bring the source light through each of the layers, dissolving each one with thanks back into the light coming through, until it reaches your body today.

Radiating Have the white light radiate fully all through your body combining with the light already there. There may be a moment of mingling where the light you have found mixes with the light which was already within you, but don't stop there. Continue to radiate the light right through every cell of your body and beyond your skin line so that you are shining out light into the world around you, into the universe even.

Do a 'feel check'. How do you feel? Is there anything else to do right now before you stop? If so, you can either do it now, following the same process as before, or you can choose to do it later, in which case tell your system when you will resume the process. Ask yourself, after this process, on a scale of 1 to 10, how much of you is now present and fully radiating. How much of your energy have you found? How much more of you is there to find in future sessions?

When you're working alone

When we're working with clients, it's relatively easy to educate the system, deal with whatever comes up and have the flexibility to respond and find another way if things seem to get stuck. There are a few things it might be useful for you to know, though, before you start this work alone.

• You can speak to the different parts of you telepathically, or by speaking aloud. You might find the latter preferable as it may help you differentiate between the different elements, and also to clarify your thinking. Be receptive to whatever thoughts come into your mind as answers. Even if these thoughts initially seem strange, or you feel you want to reject them, explore them further. Everything is already part of your energetic structure, so don't worry if what you discover initially is something you think of as 'unpleasant' or 'bad'. Just as in dreams, not everything is as it seems at first encounter. Remember, inside everything is pure light. Everything else, no matter what form it takes, is simply a protective layer, also made of light, and it needs to be dissolved back into pure light.

- If you get negative answers, say thank you and ask what the positive intention of the negative answer is. At this point you can educate the part about your understanding of the important role it has played and the necessity of its release now.

- You may find it helpful to write notes of the different layers of energy you encounter, so you can be sure to dissolve all layers when you bring the light through. Or you might like to audio-record your session so that you can go back and listen to it later to see if there are any loose ends you would like to revisit in a later session. It is not a problem if you forget to work on something. It is quite likely that it will resolve itself as you begin to radiate the light. If not, and there's still something to resolve, it will almost certainly make itself known in a later session.

- Always acknowledge and speak respectfully to your system. Thank each aspect of yourself at all times for the job it has been doing. Remember, everything in your system has always acted in its/your best interest, often just to make sure it has survived, even if you are now able to help it find a better way.

- Tears should always be viewed positively. They are an indication that you have found something important, and they are a natural expression of emotional release. Or you may be crying the tears of something in you which is joyful and relieved to be found. Some people cry more than others, some cry more on one occasion than on another, and some don't cry at all. Whichever category you come into is fine.

- If at any stage you are getting stuck in your questioning or you feel you are getting out of your depth, just ask your system where you are and what you need to do next and in what sequence. Try taking a bird's eye view of the situation, or ask your system if it can shortcut the process to get to the light more quickly. Or ask 'the part of me that knows' what you should do next. Your system can educate you! At any point, you can simply stop the process, either to resume again later or to get some professional help. When we release something, just as with lancing a boil, there may be a short period of discomfort while healing takes place – or as the next part makes itself known. However, any work you do is step in the right direction.

Susan's story

Susan was completely stressed out. She was in the middle of organising a conference and didn't really have time for a session with Eileen and Clive, but did it as part of the agreed process of writing this book. Although a part shows up as someone from a past life, it is a fairly straightforward example of how the process works. It is written from her point of view as the client. Although the session was totally guided by Eileen and Clive, their words are omitted here for brevity, as are all Susan's hesitations and 'don't knows' and attempts not to admit to what was going on!

As I sat down at the beginning of the session I was almost immediately aware of a pain in the middle of my back that seemed to have been there for ages but which I hadn't consciously noticed until that moment.

I acknowledged it and thanked it for its job, at which point it immediately became much more painful and seemed to be dragging me down. My shoulders were bowed under the weight of something which turned out to be a chain, like a mayoral chain of office. I asked how long it had been there. 'A very long time.' Before I was born or after? 'Before.' (I really really don't want to say this! I am not a person who has past life experiences. I must be making it up!) I look down to see what I am wearing. The overall impression is of green and brown. I can particularly feel my shoes which are of a very soft leather. I'm a man.

What year is it? '1654.' (I don't want to say that!)

Where am I? 'In Landau, in Germany.' (Is there a place called Landau? I think there is. I must have heard it somewhere. I'm making it up.)

Who am I? I'm a sort of chief, like a mayor. I'm a Burgermeister. I'm the Burgermeister of Landau.' (I still to this day don't know if Landau had a Burgermeister in 1654, but it doesn't matter. What happened next does.)

What kind of man is he? He's wonderful. Very hard-working, kind, tolerant, wise, conscientious. He loves the city and its people. His whole life is dedicated to doing his best for them. He's exactly the sort of person you'd like to have looking after the interests of a city, the sort of person you'd like all politicians to be. And he was wearing the 'mayoral chain of office' around his/our neck. And he too was being weighed down by it and the responsibility of looking after a whole city and so many people.

I introduced myself and told him it was 2002. He seemed surprised, and I realised that what he really wanted to know about was Landau. I told him that as far as I knew it was still a thriving city and that it had presumably managed to keep going after his death. At this point I reached for the tissues as I suddenly realised that I don't have to do everything myself. Not everything is my responsibility. Other people can do things and everybody is responsible for themselves. (This was a lesson I've had to learn before.)

I looked again at 'my Burgermeister'. He was so nice. I could see him from the outside – he had twinkly eyes and a lovely smile. At the same time I could feel what it was like to be him. He was so wise and caring.

I asked him if he would like to unite his energy with mine. What would each of us gain? I already knew that I would gain all his positive attributes which made him such a good leader. He would gain the chance to be alive again and to use his skills – and to experience the modern world. He seemed quite excited about that.

So I looked inside him and saw pure light radiating out from the very centre of his being. I invited 'him' to unite with me, and immediately I found myself looking around the room 'with new eyes', looking at a modern world from the point of view of someone from the past. At that moment too the sun came out – it had been quite cloudy all day till that point. The room almost sparkled with sunlight. I could feel 'his' light and mine mingling and merging and become the same light which was permeating every part of me and shining out into the room – and beyond. Although I could (and can) remember him vividly, he no longer existed. Somehow he had become part of me. There was just me, feeling wonderful. The word that comes to mind is 'benign'. It was a very good state from which to organise a conference!

As you can see, there was no great mystique about accessing a past life experience*, and it was not important to the process whether Susan was really a Burgermeister in a past life, whether she accessed the life someone else lived, or whether the Burgermeister was a metaphoric way of delivering information Susan needed to know. Some people get them, some don't.

* See Chapter Twelve for a our views on past life experiences.

Chapter Eight

The Unconscious Equation

As Eileen worked with clients, she became curious about why some clients took much longer than others to achieve their objectives, why a few never did, and why some initially held on to apparently irrational behaviour which was clearly doing them harm.

One client with a drinking problem would hold down a good job in the week, but at weekends would become falling down drunk. Waking in the morning, sometimes finding himself in the gutter, he would, for a moment realise that he was still alive and feel good, thankful. Then his shame would build and the drinking pattern was repeated. That momentary positive feeling was achieved through a negative process. The sequence seemed to be that he had to hold on to shame, and the drinking pattern so that he could feel momentarily alive.

Crazy? Well it makes some sense in an illogically logical way. With some people, there seemed to be a big part of them which needed to hold on to the protective pattern which resulted in the negative behaviour in order to achieve something they perceived as a positive benefit – even if it had considerable negative 'side effects'. And if you think about it, it's something we all know about.

It is certainly a common occurrence for a child to behave 'badly' in order to get the attention they don't get (often after the birth of a sibling) when they're good. Even negative attention is better than no attention. Presumably you do not enjoy being ill, but when you are ill, don't you at some level enjoy not being expected to do anything as you rest in bed and receive a certain amount of sympathy and pampering? It's not that big a step to imagine someone becoming seriously and genuinely ill as a consequence of some part of their non-conscious mind realising that they get more attention when they're ill than when they're healthy. The point is that most of us do it to a greater or lesser degree, but we do it unconsciously, and until we discover what is going on, it can interfere with attempts to overcome negative behaviour.

The Unconscious Equation is a way of expressing this non-conscious reasoning: holding onto 'x' negative behaviour with a positive intention produces some positive results but with negative consequences.

Reading another person's equation may just look like a bunch of words, but their effect on the person can be literally life changing. Lara (see Lara's story on page 125) discovered in her fifth session with us that she was holding on to struggle (negative behaviour), a pattern that she had adopted from her Yorkshire grandfather, with the positive intention of being the best she could be and feel loved. Once she realised this, she observed herself between her sessions setting up hurdles for herself, making life difficult, making mistakes, messing up relationships, and generally making life hard. She laughed all week at her new awareness and was very ready to find a new way of getting love.

Rueful laughter often accompanies the unraveling of the Unconscious Equation as people realise how they maintain chronic negative strategies and behaviours in order to try to reach a positive goal, and in falling short blame it on something or somebody outside themselves – God, parents, teachers. Trapped in this behaviour, we might then rationalise it and say things such as *'struggle is good, it makes me a better person, it helps me understand others, no pain, no gain, after all'*. It can be painful to see the look on someone's face as it dawns on them that they have wasted a good part of their life following a strategy that is not getting them what they really want. The emotions range from incredulity, a wry smile or perhaps sadness, but then there's usually a positive shift and desire to find a better way. The key is to give the person the opportunity to make a new choice, and to make sure that a greater proportion of them is committed to the new choice than to the old.

We work together with the client as they build their Unconscious Equation on a piece of paper. The examples on the following pages show how we helped people to define their equation.

---

* If you want to answer some of these questions for yourself, do the early exercises in the Wholeness Programme (starting on page 144), and Exercise 17 on page 165.

The starting point is to get answers to the following questions:

Where are you currently? What is your Present State? What is your Desired Outcome for this work? How close to that outcome are you on a scale of 1 to 10? What are you holding on to which is stopping you? What are your chronically-held negative emotions? – These chronic negative deposits, CNDs, are a healthy response to something being held, hidden, lost or missing (see page 30). – *What is the positive intention of holding on to these CNDs?* – There have to be some, or why would they keep behaving in this way?– *What do you fear you would lose by losing the negative behaviour or the CNDs?* – There is usually an unconscious fear, even if they know they will gain their outcome, and if at first they think they will lose nothing. – *What are all the negative results, including feelings, which derive from holding on to the CNDs?*

The next step in defining the equation is to have the client write down what they would like to have in place of each of the negative emotions – their 'replacement CNDs'. Then, after they release the held energy, they can define a different strategy for getting to the positive intention while keeping the positive results of the negative behaviour.

Our job is then to find the place or places in the client that have been holding the pattern in place, so they can release and integrate any trapped energy.

Simin's Unconscious Equation

Simin first came to Eileen because she felt desperate and suicidal. A beautiful but shy and withdrawn young women of 30 who was holding down a good job in the business world, she had developed a relatively positive front to present to the world when she was at work. Getting her to answer questions was like pulling teeth and her voice was very quiet. Our graduates from that year's course remember her agreeing to be a demonstration model for the group as her second session, and how she sat at the front facing Eileen, her body like a pretzel, with arms, legs, everything crossed and every answer being whispered painfully. At the end of the course, some five months later, in walked a radiant, laughing, confident beauty, who lit up the room as she described her new life. She has since moved from commerce to teaching children, with choice in who to date and with a very new outlook on her increasingly vibrant life. What follows is a summary of what happened in her fifth and sixth sessions.

Simin is clearly benefitting from her sessions. She no longer feels suicidal, she is gaining in confidence, but she still has negatie feelings she would like to resolve. She says, 'I feel there's a disconnect between me and the rest of the planet' (and with the rest of herself as well). We have an 'above/below' to work with ('me' is clearly off the planet), and we find a teenager and another younger self to work with (Simin was 30 at the time of the session). We find that her suicidal feelings, feeling bleak and that life was pointless were coming from unintegrated energies which were 'existing', but were unable to be fully alive as part of her. We begin the Unconscious Equation work by defining her Present State and Desired Outcome.

Present State: *anxiety, tension, sadness, apathy, anger and fear*

Desired Outcome: *inner calm*

We then start filling in the chart to define her Unconscious Equation. As she states each CND, we ask specific questions about each one, for example, *What's the positive intention of holding onto anxiety? What's important about holding on to tension? What are you afraid you'd lose by letting go of sadness? If what you are aiming for is peace, are you getting it?*

When all the items have been explored, Simin is helped to write a one-line summary of her Unconscious Equation: *Holding onto my CNDs enables me to see the 'truth'.*

E *What is the truth?*

S *Truth is the future Simin with inner calm.*

So Simin is staying anxious, tense, sad, apathetic, angry and fearful in order to be calm and peaceful, finding direction and purpose in life, truth. The negative consequences are still in evidence: she is moody, purposeless and deprived of sleep.

Simin*	CNDs	Positive intent	Positive Results		Negative Consequences
	(-)	(+)	(=)	(+)	(-)
	anxiety	understanding			mood swings
	tension	'truth'			
	sadness				sleep problems
	apathy	direction		I learn	have no purpose
	anger	purpose in life			
	fear	calm, secure			
Unconscious Equation: Holding onto my CNDs = truth.					

We then look at her CND Replacements. What would she like to replace each CND with? She crosses out the original word and writes her preferred alternative.

~~anxiety~~	clarity	~~apathy~~	commitment
~~tension~~	relaxation (inner)	~~anger~~	understanding
~~sadness~~	joy	~~fear~~	calm, secure, comfortable, peace

We help with positive questioning again: *If you want peace and you are not getting it, what other positive feeling could replace anxiety and still give you peace? What in you has been holding on to this strategy? Where does it live? Inside or out?*

There were many smiles of recognition and understanding during the process, but after doing some integration work and coming up with an alternative strategy, Eileen asked, *'Are you ready to make a commitment to this?'*

S *Not yet.*

E *Next time?*

S *Maybe.*

Finding the equation doesn't guarantee an immediate shift and the client may need further help to make a new choice. However, this session felt like an important turning point for her, and just before she left, she said, *'Yes, I learned something'*.

---

* Just as we were in the final stages of preparing this book we received a postcard from Simin: *'I've moved to Brighton and am getting stuck into my new teaching career at a rather challenging comprehensive. It's lots of fun and I love being by the sea.'*

The first thing Simin said when she arrived for her next session (15 Jan 2002) was *I've been very calm.*' Note that just by finding the equation and understanding its implications, the change can begin, even without conscious commitment to any process. Leaving the client to spend a week or so noticing just how the equation is working in practice can help prepare them for fully undoing the energetic pattern behind it.

Helen's Unconscious Equation

Helen's completed Unconscious Equation chart looked like this:

Replacements	CNDs	Positive intent		Positive Results	Negative Consequences
(-)	(-)	(+)	(=)	(+)	(-)
self acceptance	~~torment~~	*so I don't get hurt*		*I stay still*	*feel hellish*
	~~fear~~	*stay safe*			*don't have peace*
		peace			*don't feel confident*

Unconscious Equation: *Holding on to fear and torment = having peace.*
It is obvious one cannot feel tormented and be at peace at the same time.

Mindy's Unconscious Equation

We discovered inside Mindy her teenager self who was still on Prozac. The replacement for her Unconscious Equation was her happiness, something with which she was unfamiliar and which was hidden in deep blackness, in a void, inside her chest.

Replacements	CNDs	Positive intent		Positive Results	Negative Consequences
		(-)	(+)	(=) (+)	(-)
happiness	~~anxiety~~	*feel safe*		*familiar*	*I'm never sure*
	~~tension~~				*feel disappointed*
	~~unsure~~				

Unconscious Equation: *Holding on to anxiety, etc = feeling safe.*
Mindy learns she can't feel really safe if she holds on to her CNDs.

Janet's Unconscious Equation

It turned out that the Unconscious Equation was being held by Janet's father. Janet was holding him inside her and he was holding everyone distant in her life (including Eileen). The replacement was love, his love, which then radiated through Jane and expanded inside and outside her, transforming her into a fully loving human being.

Replacements	CNDs (-)	Positive intent (+)	(=)	Positive Results (+)	Negative Consequences (-)
love (father's love)	~~hurt~~ ~~misery~~ ~~unfeeling~~ ~~blocked~~	hold people away stay safe feel sorry for me love myself		I am me	no relationship lonely numb

Unconscious Equation: *Holding on to hurt and misery = feeling loved.*

Thomas's Unconscious Equation

To find Thomas's replacement, love, meant finding what was not loved. The job of this part was to mess things up when they were going well in order to test him. When Thomas understood his Unconscious Equation we were able to transform this part into a trusting, discerning, loving radiance.

Replacements	CNDs (-)	Positive intent (+)	(=)	Positive Results (+)	Negative Consequences (-)
love	~~sad~~ ~~scared~~ ~~lonely~~ ~~insecure~~ ~~unloved~~	get attention (I crave it)		not to make mistakes (I make mistakes now when I feel OK)	drink sexual exploits push people away illness

Unconscious Equation: *Holding on to sad, scared, etc = getting attention, feeling loved.*

Jack's Unconscious Equation

Jack's replacement is happiness, but this means choosing between an extramarital relationship and family life. Until he can find his inner happiness, he will continue to find both relationships unsatisfactory.

Replacements	CNDs	Positive intent		Positive Results	Negative Consequences
	(-)	(+)	(=)	(+)	(-)
happiness	fear	bring me		big house	stay dissatisfied
	pain	everything		lots of money	frustrated
	resentment	to struggle			tortured
	jealousy	to succeed			conflicted
	guilt				happy with
	feel inadequate				money
	remain non-				see the negative
	committal				side of any choice

Unconscious Equation: *Holding on to fear, etc = feeling happy.*

The fact that there is so much similarity between the different Unconscious Equations is because when we get down to it, we do all have very similar basic needs and emotions, and the importance of the Unconscious Equation is to get to the bottom line, so the absurdity of the holding strategies shows up clearly. The way these strategies are played out in life, though, may be very different and each person's process, while following a similar pattern, has very different content.

Chapter Nine

Negative Dependency Syndrome

Having established and understood the Unconscious Equation, clients still need to choose to make the changes in their lives. The degree to which they are able to do this very much depends on how much of their energy is invested in protection and is dedicated to holding on to the negative behaviour, and how much is able to commit positively in the present to move towards a state of wholeness, of being. As we have seen with Simin, though, sometimes just the realisation can start the process.

It is not always enough to know consciously that there are alternatives. If the person is steeped in a belief system where this is 'just the way things are', or if the political or social environment is perceived to be keeping the person at the level of pure survival, the benefits of the negative behaviour may well seem to outweigh the perceived effort involved in making a change. More importantly the reason this feels an effort is that more of their energy is invested in the old way of being with its (few) positive benefits than is invested in the possibility of change. Effectively this has become an addiction to the negative behaviour, to being a victim (it's not my fault or responsibility), or creating negative scenarios. At the level of identity it defines who they are and they are scared of 'losing themselves' if they make too profound a change. We call this addiction the 'Negative Dependency Syndrome' (NDS), and the following are some examples of the NDS at work, with the underlying unconscious decision.

- Dropped out from university and life: *'I want to be the best failure in the world; at least that will get my parents' attention.'*

- Long term emotional and mental problems: *'I want to get mentally sick, be crazy, have a lobotomy and be a vegetable, and then my family will understand how I felt.'*

- Life long physical problems: *'I don't want to be well. I would have to look after myself and that takes too much effort.'*

- Drug taker: *'That ideal self is not me. I cannot be that person. No-one would recognise me and I would lose all my friends.'*

We can try everything we know to have the person see a possible alternative future, but until we find what part of them and how much of their energy is devoted to protecting itself, which gives rise to the negative behaviour, and unless it will engage with its adult self or us, we have to step back. The part, frequently in the form of a younger self, has to indicate at least a willingness to first connect with the facilitator and the rest of its system, and then to want to engage and integrate. Sometimes we watch as, almost despite themselves, the adult takes up the posture of the defiant young self – arms crossed, chin up, lips pursed. We have to enable that inner child to see that the future with its energy integrated with the present self is better than being trapped and unexpressed in the past, with the resulting feelings.

The other possible obstacle is that the part really wants the change and the adult in the chair says they do too, but the adult is simultaneously holding an unconscious fear about what they believe will happen if the younger self is released and integrated. This fear has to be brought to the surface and the flaw in the argument brought to light.

Sometimes, the adult is not willing to choose a new path or it may not be 'the right time' – perhaps the person has to really get stuck in the mire or be in a life-threatening situation before he or she will decide it is worth making changes. Here are quotes from some who have yet to take their next steps, having decided not to continue with sessions:

'I keep myself in a straitjacket because I'm afraid of being so different in a powerful way. I'd be lonely.'

'Life (sadness, anger, loneliness, resentment, blame, selfishness, worry and fear) feels safe, familiar and predictable.'

'I made a mistake, lost my marriage and my job. I can't (won't) forgive myself.'

'My community will not accept me if I change and become who I truly am.'

'I am not going to let you help me, as that would be giving in.'

However some of our apparent failures, did have happier endings. The following is feedback from people that we sent away as they were not making the progress they said they wanted. Obviously at some level something had improved:

'Thank you. Living well is the best revenge.'

'I got a job in Burger King and I am back at college – I can be a success now.'

'I am doing typing work and I have stopped blaming my parents.'

The best tools we have are to help the person, and/or that part of them that holds the equation in place, and to work with their view of the world and their inner experiences to find a flaw in their 'arguments' or some willingness to experiment with something new. If they will not look or cannot listen, we may not be the people to help them, or they may have to fall further before they can come up. Their life is working to some degree and, while it does, they may choose to maintain their control mechanisms. We can find it difficult to accept, but we have long since realised that we may be cast in the role of authority figures by them so they can, once again, flex negative muscles. Fortunately this happens less and less often and we can usually spot it coming.

We never give up on a person while they are willing to work and, sometimes, a client will teach us that what they want is just to be listened to or supported. One client taught Eileen 'hug therapy'. Eileen had asked the client to move from her chair to the footstool next to Eileen so she could look back at herself. Suddenly the 'technique' changed and the next thing Eileen knew was that the client's head was on her chest. That's all she wanted for the best part of half a year, although occasionally Eileen did manage to slip in a bit of work. She had never had a mother's love.

There is also the question of timing. Usually when somebody finds a part of them and asks whether this is the right time to integrate, it says 'yes'. We ask 'why now'? It answers 'because you found me'. However, the person's system has its own timing and, for some, the finding may just be a first step, and the system needs time to integrate the current understanding before they are ready to move towards full integration. Ultimately, we know that the light wants to be found and released, as do all parts and layers, and it may have to burst through in some other way to get the person's attention. We look forward to the day when we can help people achieve wholeness before negative symptoms make their lives so difficult that they are forced to seek the help they need to grow and evolve.

Chapter Ten

The cultural straitjacket

Being all that you can be would seem to be a most desirable objective but sometimes there are cultural implications or a person's own belief systems which need to be taken into account. If there is pressure from the culture to conform, or if there is a belief that it is wrong to be an individual or to raise oneself up in a hierarchy, eg where men are seen as being above women, the journey to wholeness may have specific cultural roadblocks to contend with. Whatever form these limiting beliefs or limiting social or religious norms take, we refer to them as the 'cultural straitjacket'.

Cultural heritage – what it takes to be different

So often, our culture, our religious beliefs, our community is what we look to for our sense of identity. I am English, a Baptist, a Muslim, an American, a Northerner, a Villager, a Light-worker, an Arsenal supporter. Each of these helps to define both who one is and who one is not. Saying that at our roots we are all the same will produce nods of understanding, but what does it mean? It is only when a person has the experience of reaching source and radiating, filled with that light, that they truly experience the deep sense of connectedness, and then can truly value the surface level differences. Until then, there is much to do to help people move beyond the bigotry and injustice meted out in the name of cultural identity. Again, the outer behaviours mirror back what is happening on the inside. Where are the bigot, the judge, and the fear of strangers in each of us? The cultural straitjacket occurs where the effects of a belief system or way of life are so ingrained that there is a fear that by becoming a total radiating being, one will somehow no longer be recognisable or acceptable to one's group, one's family or one's friends. It's easier to fit in. Yet our soul, our body, our being aches to be fully expressed. The irony is that when we allow ourselves to actually be all that we are, that is when we find peace, a sense of aceptance and a belonging.

John's story

John came to us for coaching and for three months we worked to help him build his confidence and self-esteem in an environment where there is little management development or praise, and where bullying managers have been allowed to prevail. Part of John's strength comes from the fact that he is prepared to go beyond the cultural norms of the business. But his challenges do not end there.

He has two children, a girl and a boy, both of whom have learning disorders. His wife comes from an ethnic background that does not value women as much as men. Her parents do not acknowledge her as she has married outside her community, and they did not attend the wedding. They will help by looking after the male child, but have nothing to do with the girl. How must that child feel? What has she done with her emotions in order to cope? What effect will the rejection of her as a young child have had on the wife's energy system? What effect will that have had on her babies in the womb? How might they have protected themselves as a foetus? As she faces emotional and psychological problems of her own, what is the outlook for John? What sort of future does he have?

Fortunately, as John strengthened, he began to move beyond the struggle where he was just coping, and started to take action. Where previously he had tried to protect his family but was in denial, now he was taking steps to get help for his family as well as for himself.

Robin's story

Robin lived on a council estate with his elderly mother. He had never married and daily he experienced taunts and even violence from people living on the estate. His only choice, he thought, was to leave the estate, leave his mother, who would not leave, and find the freedom he craved.

Doing his inner work led him to discover that he could feel and be free living exactly where he lived. The bullying stopped, the violence on the estate melted away. When a person does their integration the sun comes out, even in the greyest of skies. We truly can be the creators of our universe!

Personal development within religious constraints

Clive has worked a lot with clients from ultra-orthodox religious communities, and Eileen with people from many faiths. It can be useful to have a working knowledge of the social and religious customs so as to be able to understand the meaning of what the client is saying (although you can always get the information by asking). But what is even more important is to be able to map what is going on inside the person in order to understand what that person can achieve and to be able to translate our understanding into a message that their belief system allows them to receive.

Malcolm's story

Malcolm had come for several sessions and was wondering why he would progress, feel better for a while, and then seem to fall back with recurring physical symptoms. We were wondering the same thing. He had warned us that while our model was excellent for helping to find blocks, it was limited because it dealt with the metaphysical, and that the spiritual realm, G-d's realm (his religion does not allow him to say or write the name of the almighty), was beyond anything that we could fully understand – a belief he held so deeply, he was clearly unwilling to question it. The idea of G-d himself coming down and residing within him did not fit with his beliefs. He could believe in his own over-soul, he could believe in the light of G-d and His spiritual presence, but not in becoming fully unified with G-d himself.

His intense devotional activity during the several times of prayer and the other daily observances create an intense focus, which, in our terms, can project energy out of the body. In one session, working on the recurring physical symptoms, we noticed an upward gesture and a touching of the third eye (centre of forehead). We had him use his inner vision to look upwards. He saw a ladder, Jacob's ladder, with angels climbing up and down. We asked him who had put it there?

M *I did.*

E *Who or what is at the top? What would happen if you reached the top?*

M *I would see G-d, be in G-d's presence.*

E *Is it possible to reach the top?*

M *No. That is perfection and I can only aspire to climb and improve myself.*

Using the Unconscious Equation he saw that he was holding on to struggle in order to perfect himself, to feel good, and that he had to fall back down the ladder (keep his symptoms) so as to continue the process. The negative consequence was to be in pain.

E *Whose energy is the ladder made of? Whose energy is G-d made of?*

M *My energy.*

He knew this, since this could not actually be the G-d that he prayed to. He brought the light out of the ladder, 'G-d' and the whole scene and down into himself. It was useful to know the rules about creating idols or false images, since we could agree that what he had done in his System was, in our terms, to create the image of a false inner G-d. If the presence or light of the true G-d had tried to come into him it would be blocked, which was the case. The light came into him and he experienced some relief. However, his symptoms persist. Will he ever fully accept our understanding of the light's journey to know itself and stop the process of projecting energy above the body? We wonder how this would fit within his community, devotional practices and belief system. However, he confirms the benefits, the learning and the strengthening that he has received from RAPSI.

Legacies of past lives

There are occasions when the beliefs of a person from a past life existence permeate the present life. As well as making it difficult for the client to function well, it can make our work with the client a bit more complicated too as we need to understand and acknowledge the norms of the past life and find ways to update the person to the social norms of today in a way they can accept. The trick seems to be to discover and work directly with the past life person, within their own set of understandings while responding honestly and appropriately. The facilitator always needs to build a relationship, not only with all aspects of the client, but also with all other people who appear in the past life. We find it very useful sometimes that there are two of us working together!

Jonas's story

Jonas was not easy to work with. There were long silences and it was difficult to get him to open up. There seemed to be some topics, particularly his relationships, that he was unwilling to talk about freely and we began to wonder why he had bothered to call. Eileen also noticed that when she, a female, asked him questions, he seemed almost not to listen, but when Clive reworded or repeated the same question, he would hear him and reply more easily. Jonas, we discovered was carrying a past life as a Monk who had made a vow of silence and a vow of celibacy. Before we could release his trapped energy, we needed to help Jonas make telepathic contact with various people involved in his decision to be a monk: his Abbot to whom the vows had been given, the Monk's Father who had sold him to the Abbot when he was seven years old, and his Mother who had been unable to stop him.

It took a lot for the Monk to eventually forgive his Father and Mother, discover his own feminine side to balance his zealous self-denial. He also had to ask the Abbot to release him from his vows. No wonder Clive was having to 'translate' what Eileen was saying.

Matthew's story

Matthew was on our first US workshop in California and he was very undecided about whether he really wanted to be there. He chose to stay for the first day and as we worked with the group, it became evident that he was becoming agitated. As we worked with him, he sensed something hovering overhead and heard a voice. It was the energy of a man from a past life who had taken his son's life as part of a group suicide pact. The man was one of the elders who had been appointed to take the lives of some 900 people on the top of Mount Masada in what is now southern Israel, rather than let them be killed or taken into slavery by the Romans. After three years of siege, although the encampment had provisions and water to hold out for another three years, the Romans were finally completing a ramp up the side of the mountain in order to take the encampment. Anticipating a clearing of the event through Mathew, we were surprised when other participants began to describe aspects of the event as they also sensed/saw/experienced this shared past life. Several had died on Masada and described the buildings on the top. (We went to Masada after this and saw for ourselves how accurate they were.) One was a Roman Centurion climbing the ramp, one a shepherd boy on the plain below and one a woman (Clive's own experience) who had hidden with her two daughters and was taken into slavery. Eileen had no feeling of involvement in the past event. We needed to help heal not only the anguished father, but the other 900 or more souls as well.

We later wondered about this being a form of 'group hysteria' or other explanations such as a shared soul stream. Only one person in the workshop was Jewish by birth and upbringing and only knew vaguely that there was something in history about a place called Masada. None of the others had heard of it, at least consciously. This was a powerful healing experience where we worked with what the event required including the souls forgiving each other for the decision that was taken on Mount Masada. Interestingly the man who had felt a kinship with a Roman soldier failed to show up the next day.

Hilda's story

In an introductory workshop many years ago, Eileen was working with Hilda who suddenly saw two disembodied eyes in front of her. When she was instructed to look into them, they took her to a death camp in Poland and to a Nazi officer who had raped and killed a woman. Much to Eileen's surprise, Hilda identified Eileen as the officer and herself as the woman. Rather than Hilda talking to the officer and the woman within her own system, Eileen took the role of the officer and apologised for what he had done.

While the 5Rs – Recognition, Relationship, Reconciliation, Release and Radiating – suggest an orderly step-by-step approach, it is rarely that simple, but it is certainly not 'normal' to find oneself cast as one of the participants in an event. However the facilitator's job is to do whatever needs doing and to react intuitively, naturally and appropriately. Eileen shared the deep feeling of peace which followed the healing.

Clive has also worked with more than one client who has identified his energy as being linked to the male in one or more lifetimes and who had caused them hurt or worse. Occasionally there was recognition by him that this 'felt right', but without direct personal experience, he, again, simply apologised in the role of the person they were seeing. These moments tends to be quite poignant.

Cultural gender differences

Harriet's story, which is told in full on page 104, is an extreme example of the tragic consequences of cultural insularity and conditioned constraints, as a result of which tragedies still occur all too frequently in the news today. It was the rejection by the parents and community of the son's fiancée that led to the murder of the woman and her three-year-old daughter by her fiancé's parents. Harriet was feeling the heaviness and dread of the events and the people. It was the caste system, which defined the girl as being unworthy to marry the son as she was English, and it was the shame brought on the parents that fuelled the violent and cruel act. To Harriet, these were actual people from her present life and their feelings were ingrained in her, though she had no previous conscious knowledge of this. Part of the healing involved acceptance by the community of the terrible wrong that was done and what needed to be learned. Harriet was carrying all the cultural baggage as well as the energy of the people involved.

Boys and girls growing up in, say, the English public school system, or girls growing up in a number of very strict religious cultures, learn to inhibit, hide and eventually suppress their respective feminine or masculine energies. Signs of sensitivity can lead to bullying – which frequently leads to the victims becoming bullies in their turn. Girls (usually) can be punished for wanting to have a career. Stepping over cultural lines can lead to expulsion or even death. What happens to the energetic expression of small children in such an environment? It becomes inhibited, and the children create all sorts of inner mechanisms to ensure that they remain acceptable to their family and community, with who knows what effects on their inner selves.

Bruce's story

Bruce was a businessman who wanted to move to the next level in his company and become head of his department with directorial responsibility. He was great at his job, good with the customers, liked and respected by his sales team, but was somewhat confrontational with his peers. In a six-hour intensive session, he roleplayed becoming the Sales Director and presenting to the board, reviewed his scores on a scale of leadership competencies, and defined his ideal future self. We also had him assess what would stop him getting there. Doing some personal exploring, he found his six-year-old self behind him, sitting on a wall with his grandfather in Yorkshire. Grandfather was giving his opinion of work, schooling, the south of England and life in general. Bruce realised, as he looked further back, that his Mum and Dad were also there.

He sensed that his failure to go to university, his narrow focus and competitive way of dealing with his peers all stemmed from holding (unconsciously) his grandfather's beliefs and not wanting to betray his roots. Like a long rubber band, he had stretched as far forward as he could go in his career. Until he could recover the energy from his past and bring it to his present, he was curtailing his prospects.

Five years on, after a successful spell as UK Sales Director, Bruce has been appointed European Sales Director.

Beliefs can come in all forms. Each of us has our own understanding of how the universe works and our place within it. If that understanding is strongly held, then anything which challenges it risks being rejected out of hand. That holds true too for people with a strong belief in how therapy should be conducted although we've found that 'truth' is typically recognisable. We are aware that some of the things we have written in this book might go against some of the accepted beliefs of the world of therapy and personal development community (if there is such a thing). But that's why we have written this book. If our learnings are different, we want to share them. Not for our own sake, but because it is how the inner journey of our clients (nearly 2000 to date) has unfolded. If someone wants to take the RAPSI journey, then they have to be willing to open their mind to new possibilities. This book gives a taste of what is possible. Experiencing a facilitated RAPSI session is recommended before making a final judgement.

We salute the many courageous individuals who have looked into a future which suggests that they may have to move beyond their familiar cultural and social boundaries in order to be fully who they were meant to be, who come to believe that their radiating can be a positive beacon for others. In some cases they do need to break their cultural ties to join the increasing community who move freely through a wider world. However, many who achieve wholeness find that they are examples to others and that they are empowered to influence and help their family or community evolve.

Chapter Eleven

Integrating the observers

At the end of a session and having re-integrated a major portion of the person's energy (up and down, right and left, front and back, and 'pockets' inside the body), we always ask, several times, how the person feels, to help them become aware of their change and notice how things are different. Normal responses are 'calm, peaceful, warm', etc. Sometimes, however, as they are walking towards the door to leave, if not before, they hear another internal voice, speaking in a different tone, asking *'But will it last?'* or *'How do I maintain this?'* A questioner, doubter or controller has just made itself known. This is one of several voices or behaviours coming from energy stashes, often located in the head or out of the body, which are separate from and therefore unconnected with what is going on in the rest of the body in 'now-time'. They may see and hear what is going on, but are unable to be involved at a feeling level. The doubter/questioner is doing a positively-intentioned job of 'not trusting' almost anything it sees or hears in order to try to find certainty. (This impossible task is an example of the paradox of the Unconscious Equation – see page 55).

Doubting can include doubting what has happened in a session and over time can whittle away at the person's new-found good feelings. A controller's job is to manage things so as to keep the person on track or safe (by keeping them cut off or dumbed down), or even to make sure they fail, obviously for a positively-intended purpose.

The difficulty is that these 'observers' are a powerful part of the protective system. Although they may take the form or voice of someone else (grandfather, mother, etc), they are probably the part of you which has so far been doing the exploration. They may even identify themselves with 'you' so strongly that they think they are the only 'you', and sometimes even be unaware that the 'you' of today exists. We are now asking those parts to integrate themselves. This means engaging with the fundamentals of your belief system and some major elements of your belief system. These are some of the final pieces which need to be integrated if you are to find wholeness.

Up to the time of writing this book we have held the view that it needs a skilful facilitator to help the person locate and integrate these final pieces. We (Eileen and Clive) have had to help each other dismantle defence mechanisms rather than working alone. They were designed to protect us from harm and are often deep 'in' our blind spots, making it difficult to 'spot' them without help. They are not easy to discover, and they need to be taught – a key part of the facilitator's job is to find and then help these parts understand that it is only by integrating 'their' energy with 'yours' that you can be truly protected, worthy, or whatever its aim for you (and it) is.

The first job though is to locate them.

So what kinds of observers do people typically find? The names are those we have given them. The words in italics represent language, which may point to an observer doing a particular job.

A Doubter casts doubt on almost anything and was often created when there was a lot of uncertainty in childhood, typically if the child was badly let down by adults or could not trust the adults around them.
• *I'm not sure that I didn't make that up. Did I do the right thing? Did I make the right choice, the right decision? I doubt that anybody can love me? Are you sure?*

A Questioner is rarely satisfied with an answer, raises another question, analyses every situation and is a close cousin of or another facet of the doubter, but this constant questioning of oneself whittles away confidence and self-esteem.
• *What if x happens? But what about …?*

A Controller often believes that it controls everything going on in the person's system – and sometimes it does. It is usually applying a 'brake' to the system and may or may not be responsible for 'allowing' things to happen. The controller was usually set up when life was out of control, in the control of someone else, a family member or teacher, or not in the control of the person whose job it should have been, such as a parent.
• *My Mum can't cope, so I need to take control. I control myself/others. I hold*

myself back. I mustn't allow the system to feel, because to feel is to hurt and I won't get my needs met anyway. I stop myself ... I won't let myself ...

A Judge is usually an energy fragment existing at a distance, unable to engage. All it can do is judge with the aim of 'getting things right' in order to get approval, but too much self-judgement can be debilitating. Its positive intention is often to learn how to do things right or do things better, but it can have a range of critical or belittling behaviours. Where the person was judged heavily as they grew up, they may have unconsciously created their own judge as a defence mechanism.

• *If I judge myself first, they will have nothing to judge me for. I am bad, worthless, a piece of shit. I could do better. I criticise myself. I let myself down.*

A Watcher can be a 'look out', whose job is to see danger coming, either from a forward-looking place or from behind, where it tends to be more active in its watching. Sometimes it is situated in the centre of the forehead or behind the body. It stays awake and may never sleep, which may affect the person's sleep patterns. No wonder the person gets tired. Now wonder too that he/she gets into trouble or hangs out with 'the wrong sort'. The watcher is always looking out for danger – looking for trouble. And it finds it.

• *I stay alert. I can't sleep. I see things coming. I watch myself ... I keep an eye out/open.*

A Witness can be looking down, or standing back, to one side or in front. Its job is to stay separate, uninvolved and bear witness to the person's life. It may be quiet, silently watching, waiting to help.

• *I see myself doing ... I notice my thoughts, my emotions. I am not my body. I seem to be an onlooker in my life. I feel lonely. I have no sense of belonging. I yearn for connectedness. The material world is all an illusion anyway.*

A Scale-holder tries to maintain the balance between right and left, like the scales of justice.It maintains the gap between different parts of oneself which may mirror conflict between one's parents in childhood.

• *My now score is 5 out of 10. I sit on the fence. I'm feeling so-so, 50/50. I feel caught in the middle.*

A Higher Self can be something of the self which has been ejected or has 'wandered off' because of some painful experience (something all observers have in common), or it may be a learned or conditioned part of the energetic structure. A higher self may also be part of the self which is at a great distance up above, and feels it is not limited by time and space, has great breadth of vision and understanding and attempts to offer wisdom and guide our life and/or lives. In fact it may not necessarily know as much as it thinks because it is so disengaged from the person, their everyday life and their needs. It almost certainly does not know about the need for all their energy to be integrated. A higher self is higher in location, but is not better than any other part or higher in any hierarchical sense. It is still powerless to do anything without being fully in the person here in the present.

Not all higher selves are magnanimous and gracious. Some are sleeping, waiting for their 'vehicle' to awaken to their existence. Some have been in body at some time in the person's life. The person's relationship with this 'higher' part of the self is not necessarily a good one, since the latter may be judging its vehicle as not being good enough or ready for its entry, not realising that its absence is part of the reason for the person's struggle and/or inadequacy. It may give profound statements, or judgements about the human condition.

- *I feel as if I am from another planet. I am not of this earth. I see everything that goes on. My home is in the stars/in heaven. I have a global view of things. I look down on myself, which is not good enough. I need to perfect myself in order to be worthy.*

Something in the basement Not everything is above ground level. An energy below the feet, and far below that, can also be waiting, observing, unused, feeling useless. The journey to find it may involve going down a shaft or well or through a dark vortex, an inner black hole, into a volcano, through water, into the core of the earth or beyond to find light.

- *I feel stepped upon. I am overwhelmed. I feel deeply depressed. I can barely keep my head above water.*

Guides, Angels, Master Teachers, God(s), Demons and the Shadow All of these (and any other 'beings' with whom we seem to make contact), in our experience, are invariably the other realms of the person's larger multi-dimensional self, and the person's learning is that these energies are meant to be embodied and their gifts manifested here in the present. Keeping them at a distance, while it might enable the person to have some special insights, is still keeping the light trapped outside the body, instead of allowing it to be fully manifested where the insight can be acted upon by all the energy. Maintaining these energies at a distance creates a dependency and is disempowering. Bringing them 'here' and radiating this light brings deep understanding and resources to empower the person.

• *I talk to God daily (even if He doesn't seem to listen). God looks after me. I can't look after msyelf. My guides tell me what to do. I am protected by the angels. I follow where (a Master Teacher/my guru) leads. I am surrounded by evil forces.*

With any observers, the aim is not to get rid of them or lose their valuable contribution, although this is usually what the person fears. What a person fears has typically already happened. If we fear losing someone's love, for example, it is often because we know subsconsciously that they no longer love us. In this case by having the energy 'out' and observing, the person does not have the full value of their contribution. The aim is to dissolve the metaphysical form into energy/light which is brought fully into the body to expand and radiate, making all of its resources fully available, all of the time.

Dark energies, or 'dark forces', can be particularly misleading as people tend to react with fear. But that's their greatest success. The light cloaks itself in darkness as a protection, but darkness is always hiding light. The Shadow can always be penetrated and dissolved.

Many people who have done a lot of personal development work are in touch with their observers and gain valuable insights from them, but as long as they are kept 'once removed', a system of communication, such as meditation, needs to be set up in order to contact them. This may be an excellent first step towards accessing their wisdom, but why not access that wisdom all the time, without any need for a communication system? Indeed, why not be the wisdom. How much more becoming that would be!

Remember, it is the cloak, the layer of protection of source that can be ignorant, sleeping, judgemental, or simply out of touch. Source itself remains waiting to be found and reintegrated so that it can radiate fully.

Tony's story

Tony came to see us, labelled 'sociopathic', having been sectioned for violent behaviour. He had largely dropped out of society, but he had saved enough money from what he deemed his menial job to undertake therapy. Sitting well away from us, he talked about his life, being *separated from my family* in Europe at an early age and becoming more and more *angry in myself* and *disruptive on the outside* (italics are his own words). He remembered little of his early years. While he was talking, he frequently touched his right temple, as he described fits of anger and the headaches from which he suffered. His overall appearance was of a powerfully-coiled spring.

Asking where he experienced the headaches, he consciously pointed to his right temple. When he looked into his right hemisphere he saw darkness, which explained that it was there to protect him and to keep him out. When asked what it was made of, it described itself as *collapsed or compressed light*. As he acknowledged its existence and its positively intended job, it lightened to reveal the entrance to a tunnel. As he travelled through the tunnel, he felt the sensation of travelling into his head, down his neck, around his shoulder, across his chest and down to his abdomen. Each ridge of the tunnel was 'formed by one of life's experiences' and he had flashes of memory, pictures, sounds and the associated feelings.

As he neared his abdomen he saw *light at the end of the tunnel* and as he approached it he had the experience of coming out of his body and rising several feet above and looking down on himself. From his position in the chair, he was now able to describe a *golden light, hovering* above him. It said it had been there from his birth and proceeded to show him the incident from its vantage point. It explained that the separation between it and him had occurred in the womb. The pressure of his mother's feelings of dread in the political situation in middle Europe relayed themselves to the energy system of the foetus. He described going through his own *big bang* and of *imploding*. He *went in on himself* and, simultaneously, part of him was ejected, *floating, a survival mechanism, should the body die*. This 'observer' was then able to describe the birth and the moment after birth when the doctor, over-tired and slightly intoxicated, cut the baby's stomach as he cut the umbilical cord. He was shown the events that followed and heard the conversations in his native tongue.

He also saw two later occasions at age two and four when he stopped breathing and nearly died. He saw people that he had never met and because many of his family were no longer alive, he initially had no means of verifying these events.

The observer, literally his 'higher self' had been trying to *communicate its feelings* to him of *loneliness and frustration*, and of *judgement*, the last two being feelings that he felt constantly. He knew that when he meditated, he reached a *place of peace* where he *no longer felt pain* and he wanted *more and more to leave my body and be there.* Through talking with this disembodied energy, he learned that by keeping the energy outside, he was maintaining the pain and was denying himself good feelings. The positive intention of this was *to help myself learn.* The irony of this was not lost on him, as his 'sociopathic' condition removed him from any possibility of interacting and learning in a positive way. It was at this point that he made a conscious and now possible, choice to change.

The 'God' that he had been praying to was this voice and disembodied energy, and, as he learned later, the permanent *state of grace* that he was seeking could not be achieved by vacating his body but by bringing the energy back from the *negative universe* into his body. The *divine essence* was *waiting for me to find it and bring it home, so that I can experience life to the full.*

He thanked the golden light and looked further into it. It gave way to blackness, like the *night sky, with stars.* He was attracted to one star and as he looked further in he saw a *pure translucent brilliant light.* He communicated with it and learned that it was the *source of your essence* and that it had been waiting to be found. He learned that he needed to invite it to return. He saw it travel first through the centre of the star, then through the middle of the blackness, through the middle of the gold, both of which dissolved into the light, and then down to his navel where it entered the tunnel. He described the sense of a *sleeve being turned inside out and of the dark walls of the tunnel dissolving back into the light.*

On the outside, it was evident that something was going on as he was trembling and his normally sallow cheeks were suffused with colour. He described *a light going on* in his right brain, and then discovered more light in the left brain. These merged and then he experienced a *shower of energy* passing through his body. From our vantage point, we literally saw him uncoil his body, his cheeks filled

81

out, the scowl disappeared and a calm look took its place. His temperature appeared to cool and he sat in apparent amazement, then leapt to his feet to hug the first human that he had touched in 30 years.

Seeing him some time later, he was jauntily dressed and had been back to his homeland where he had tracked down his remaining family and pieced together the story of his life which confirmed what he had already discovered. By 'coming home' into his physicality, he was able to 'go home' in the outer world.

Jim's story

Jim was 36 and had messed up badly in some senior positions in business. He was also failing in his personal relationship and as a provider for his family. He had been out of work for many months and felt pretty worthless. At the same time, however, outwardly he took a very superior attitude to everything and everyone, and had an amazingly laissez-faire attitude to his own behaviour, especially considering that his first marriage had failed for similar reasons. It was as if nothing mattered, all would be well. 'There was a larger picture', he said.

As we worked, he found an energy thousands of feet above his head, with a broad perspective and very little idea of the struggle Jim was having, trying and failing to be successful. He invited it to come closer. It saw him finally, floating in a sea, treading water, unable to swim to land. It realised that they were connected and the result was that Jim was picked up *by a boat which sailed towards shore.*

Afterwards, his outer world situation improved and he got a routine job, which allowed him 'freedom' in terms of his time. Since this had been his objective, he stopped coming to us. What we noticed was that this kind of 'freedom' meant that the energy was still outside him, and that he was earning very little and still had relationship issues to resolve. This 'free' energy needs to be embodied and while there is usually a fear that embodiment means containment and losing freedom, the person and the energy have to learn about the actual results of fully radiating energy (fully in, paradoxically is also fully out) and having it available at all times. This is true freedom which leads to further successes in one's life.

Jim's observer was of the 'higher', and ignorantly 'superior' kind, while actually being impotent. It and Jim will have those traits until Jim and the source light beyond that found so far agree to integrate.

Shane's story

Shane was angry and felt that he was surrounded by a 'dark evil force' (his observer) all around him which had been created when his mother attempted to abort him. This was a real experience for Shane, but was by no means the end of the story. As he communicated with the darkness, however, it became a beautiful being which dissolved into light.

S *It was created when I was aborted.*

E *Update it. Tell it that it's 1996. That you survived and are now 66.*

Shane finds a 14-year-old self inside him, in which reside the origins of some of his sexual problems. The light outside helps Shane find the darkness in the 14-year-old's sexual organs and free the light. Standing behind a door in Shane (in his chest) is a black ball. Inside that was an 18-year-old indulging in rash sexual exploits, and inside him a 13-year-old, a shy boy who preceded the discovery of sex at 14. The light inside the 13-year-old's chest was seen by the light outside, and vice versa. The inner light was that light, which became contained to protect innocence as Shane went against his religious teaching and began to 'commit mortal sin'. The energy outside was darkness which was protecting the light which had vacated his body when death, as a result of him being aborted, seemed imminent.

Shane attributed the concept of evil forces to the darkness outside, which is what he felt it was, since the attempts of the light to re-enter his body caused pressure, oppression and suggestive voices. Pressured feelings from the pure place in him (the energy of 13), which was its attempt to get his attention, produced pressure from the inside, where the only temporary release was the sexual act.

Once everything had been found, the outer energy said, *'You don't need me here any more'*, and the form dissolved into light.

S *It feels as though my heart has been bruised and it's healing, adding to the light. I have a sense of the oneness of the whole universe and I need to bring it in to the microcosm of the macrocosm.*

He is silent for about 10 minutes as he receives 'the universe'. He looks very much at peace, is deeply in himself, breathing slowly and deeply, face no longer holding even a smile, totally relaxed, serene.

E *How do you feel?*

S *Like a spaceship going through space and allowing myself to draw the energy in.* (He points to his chest area.) *I now feel deeply alive.*

Jack's story

Follow the language as Jack speaks at intervals through the session. With literal listening and the right questions, Jack was able to find everything that he needed to find in one session. (We've omitted Eileen's part here for brevity.)

My ex-girlfriend told me that she regarded me as a pain, and she 'felt obliged' to have lunch with me when I asked. She felt I was observing her instead of engaging with her fully. I need to find time and space for myself. My wife Jane relies on me for my strategic abilities. I am more observant than she is. I see the big picture. I don't want to lose that. I procrastinate (whatever the positive intention, 'watching' results in an inability to commit to or to take action). I lost myself. When I was four, I slept alone. I got up in the night and went outside and the door shut behind me. My parents didn't come to find me, even though they knew where I was. When I was bigger, I became detached. It taught me not to care. It's detached and right in front of me, like plate glass. I am behind the glass. Myself and the rest of the world are in front of it. My four-year-old is behind me, observing, behind the glass, frozen, on the back doorstep. The glass is dissolving. The me in front has come into me. Now four is completely inside me. He loves it inside and so do I, but I feel worried. My parents want the four-year-old back (he was carrying their worry and was trying to make them happy). There are two balls of energy, one in each foot. They help me walk. Actually they have had difficulty because they are shielded by blackness. They've been trying to make friends. As I look into the balls, the one in my left foot contains my future. I have been stepping on myself! It's released now and gone all through my body. In the right sphere, everything is there. Me at seven. It's making me walk around in circles. It has released. I feel well. I'm OK and really I am a good person. There is a rod still inside me. It's the 'me' bit inside the rod. The rod was hollow with a special element protected inside. I want to know I'm going to be all right. It's in my throat. It's been asking questions. It wants to be happy. There's a happy face in there, smiling so that no-one else would be unhappy. It's released. I feel proud of myself.

Apart from a seven-year-old self who had the specific job of making Jack run round in circles, Jack had two observers: a four-year-old self, frozen and passively dissociated, was the witness behind him, and a questioner in his throat.

Roy's story

Dealing with irritable bowel syndrome and spastic colitis, Roy was never far from a toilet. His life was on hold. He was not even able to give a plus score when saying how close he was to his defined outcomes. He was on a minus scale (not unknown). His case was an example of an observer energy 'in the basement'.

We saw him on the top (23rd) of a building in Los Angeles where we were borrowing an office to work in. He had braved the elevator to see us. During his work, he said that he wanted to know God and he entered inside his internal universe. At that moment a 2.5 (Richter scale) earthquake rocked the building.

Later in the session, he found a volcano and knew he had to jump into it. As he jumped in his mind's eye, a 4.2 earthquake rocked the building. We continued the session and he found the light below and brought it into his body.

His symptoms cleared and so, fortunately, did the earthquake, but we made a mental note to see our clients at ground level in future! Beyond joking, however, we know that we powerfully create and affect our world. We frequently have the experience, even on the cloudiest days, of the sun breaking through as a client finds and brings through the light. If everyone of us is of the source, then we are source, and it would be wise for us to create wisely. Integrating our fragments of energy will create the peace that we all, at some level, want to achieve.

Daniel's story

Daniel was a young man who had agreed to have a demonstration session in our training course. At one point in the session, he became aware that his indecision about his future was coming from inside, in the back of his head. He looked in using his inner eyes, but no matter how hard he tried, he could not find anything (even probing the dark – his observer was looking through his eyes from the inside and could not turn to see itself). He was asked to sit in the chair opposite and look back at an image of himself sitting on the original chair. He looked, with his eyes open, into the back of the head of the image opposite, where he saw his 14-year-old self experiencing indecision at school. He described what he saw as a dark glass tunnel, narrowing in perspective as it got further a way. A small 14-year-old figure was at the far end, totally oblivious to the existence of the young adult of today. He gently got the 14 year old's attention and felt waves of relief rushing forward to him (the adult). Once they had resolved what they would each contribute to each other, the energy of the 14 year old came into the Daniel sitting in the opposite chair. Adult Daniel glowed. Walking back to sit down in his original chair, Daniel felt the clarity and certainty which resulted from the integration – within the 14 year old had been clear light, clarity, although it had been protected and therefore withheld. Now able to look into a clear future (clarity brings clarity), Daniel could see his path and his first step in a new career. He left and last time we heard of him he was doing exceptionally well in computing.

Anna's story

A *I have a dread and fear of evil.*

This resulted in healing a past life as an Inquisitor, a Cardinal in the Spanish Inquisition. Then …

A *I feel as if I am being guided.*

E *Where from?*

A *Above.*

E *Where above?*

A *Back and to the right.**

* It is extraordinary that for 99 per cent of clients, their system is able to answer these questions very easily.

86

E   *Is that guiding coming from outside, inside or from both?*

A   *It's definitely outside me and it feels quite distant, but I also notice a twitch in my right brain, which feels familiar, when I'm channelling.*

E   *Say hello to it.*

A   *Hello.*

E   *With your outer eyes closed, tell me what you see when you look there in your right brain.*

A   *I see darkness.*

E   *Thank it for being there and look through it.*

Eileen could have gathered more information but she was moving quickly and it didn't seem necessary.

A   *There's a night sky, the heavens, the cosmos, all of it.*

E   *Thank it for being there, ask it whether it has had a function and tell me what it replies.*

A   *It has been guiding me. I have been channelling its wisdom, it's my psychic ability.*

E   *How has it felt doing that job?*

A   *Distant, removed, lonely, a bit powerless to help, only to suggest.*

E   *Have you ever felt distant, removed, lonely, and powerless?*

A   *All the time.*

E   *Well you were probably feeling its feelings. Check it out.*

A   *Yes, that's true.*

E   *Ask it what it would bring if you were able to reach the source of that energy.*

A   *Understanding, ability, comfort, a feeling of being home.*

E   *You mentioned home before and that you had wanted to leave your body, go home, into the heavens. How can your body be 'home'?*

A   *The energy wants to come home to me. I thought it was the other way round.*

E   *You realise that these questions are for your learning, not to give me information, as I already know this from past clients.*

A   *I understand.*

E   *What will you gain from the energy coming into your body?*

A   *I will feel complete and powerful in my healing work. I will be able to make some money!*

E *Good, so now look into the night sky, what do you see?*

A *Stars.*

E *Let one star catch your attention and use it as a doorway to look through.*

A *It's vast, a bright white light.*

E *Is this source, the source of light?*

A *Yes.*

E *Look still further to make sure.*

We do this to make sure the person has gone far enough and that this is not another layer.

A *It's become even brighter.*

E *Say hello to it.*

A *Hello.*

E *Ask it, did it know that you would find it today?*

A *Yes!*

E *Did it have anything to do with you coming here to see me?*

A *Yes, it told me to come.*

E *Light, how do we know that this is the right time for you to be brought in?* (Anticipating the usual answer about timing.)

A/L *Because you found me today.*

E *What have you been doing there?*

A/L *Waiting.*

E *How has that felt?*

A/L *Boring.* (A feeling that Anna had mentioned earlier.)

E *Why did you not push through from your side?*

A/L *I couldn't.*

E *Why not?*

A/L *Because of the dimensions in between.*

E *Who created those dimensions?*

A/L *I did.*

E *Why?*

A/L *It happens as part of the process of creating the human form.*

E *Have you ever been fully embodied in a human form?*

A/L *No.*

E *What does that feel like?*

A/L *Senseless.*

E *If you knew, what would it feel like to be in body?*

A/L *I don't know.*

A *Joyful!*

E *Do you know anything about Anna of today?*

A/L *We have communicated.*

E *How?*

A/L *In her mind.* (She touches the right side of her head.)

E *Will she lose her abilities to communicate telepathically if you come into her?*

A/L *No, the opposite, she will gain discernment, intuition, knowing.*

E *Can you see her?*

A/L *No.*

E *Would you like to?*

A/L *Yes.*

E *Please look through the bright white, through the star, through the night sky and tell me what you see.*

A/L *Light in a form.*

E *What does it look like?*

A/L *Like me.*

E *Lights, please say hello to each other.*

A/L *Yes.*

E *I suggest that you may want to acknowledge Anna for having the guts to journey to find you. After all she has been struggling without you.* (Struggle was something she'd mentioned earlier.)

A/L *Thank you.*

E *Are you ready to come together?*

A/L *Yes.*

E *Can you make this happen yourself?* (Sometimes it happens spontaneously.)

A/L *No.*

E *What needs to happen?*

A/L *She needs to help me.*

E *Do you know your re-entry point?*

Anna touches the right side of her head.

E *Anna, on the count of three, with your intention, draw down this vastness. As it comes, have the bright light, the star, the night sky dissolve back into the light and have it come down into you, merging with your light which we released earlier. Have it expand into every cell of you.*

A *It's coming in. Oh my God it's amazing, truly amazing. I am buzzing, all tingly. Wow. I'm hot. My skin is hot. I feel flushed.*

E *When it reaches your skin line, have it continue to expand, radiating out, as slowly as it needs, filling the room.*

A *Yes.*

E *Filling the house.*

A *Yes.*

E *Filling the village and the country.*

A *Yes.*

E *Filling the world.*

A *Oh yes.*

E *How do you feel?*

A *I feel everything. Peaceful yet ecstatic. I have found my wisdom.* (She opens her eyes.)

E *What do you see?*

A *The world is a brighter more vivid place. The colours are more vibrant.*
Later evidence of the effects of this work came as Anna began to attract more clients and felt able to charge a higher fee. She no longer needed to create the ritual of channelling as her knowing was resident within her and she was able to know things instantly. Her language about the universe changed and she became less reverential and more spiritually human!

This journey into a night sky illustrates how to integrate the 'Higher Consciousness', the 'Universal Observer'. This, or something very similar, happens so frequently that we believe that this is a universal journey that needs to be taken at some point by each person, to incorporate the energy above.

To show that the RAPSI process doesn't have to be complicated, it is interesting to note that while Susan was reading this paragraph as part of the preparation for this book, she spontaneously experienced the events described.

'I had felt quite moved by Anna's story, but when I read the paragraph about most people experiencing the 'night sky journey', I realised that I had never experienced such a journey. Without any significant conscious intent, I brought to mind an image of the night sky. Suddenly I found that I was crying and at the same time flooded with light, radiating. I felt wonderful, 'tingly', for the rest of the day.'

Chapter Twelve

Past lives and ancestral healing

We differentiate between a past life and an ancestral line.

A past life may be found where there is an energetic link to the history of an individual, a group or an event, which affects and permeates the reality of the person of today. These can be human or non-human existences. Sometimes one past life can be linked in some way to another.

An ancestral line may be found where a trait, a behaviour, a negative feeling or a symptom is carried down the bloodline, the direct ancestry, through men or women or both, and is inherited by the person of today.

Past lives

Not everyone encounters past lives, but they do seem to lie behind many presenting problems that are difficult to shift or where there is no apparent reason in this lifetime to explain the problem. We are not unique in working with past lives, however what we do with them may be different. Past life experiences can occur spontaneously and without prompting, and often they do, enough for us to 'believe' in them. They happen. Someone is on an inner journey, they look through a doorway and discover somebody who seems to be them in some way from a past life. Often they describe this person in great detail – what they look like, what they are wearing, how they and the people around them are living, the precise details of the situation in which they currently find themselves, what they are saying and how they are acting and feeling. All of this is described in the first person as if this has happened to them, just as you would describe something that happened to you when you were younger. In several cases, the information that has emerged has subsequently been found to be true, even though the person consciously knew nothing about it.

So do past lives exist? They certainly exist for the person who is experiencing them and, from our direct experience with many clients, we do not think they are metaphors. We think it quite plausible that, in this energetic continuum from subtle to gross energy, people are able to open doorways and follow their energy to real past experiences. It may well be that our fragmented energy system includes traces from our past lives, an energetic inheritance.

The important point to make, though, is that it is not necessary to believe in reincarnation in order to benefit from this part of a RAPSI journey. It doesn't matter whether you 'believe in' past lives or not. It doesn't matter whether people are genuinely 'remembering' a life their soul/energy lived before, or whether they are tapping into a vast field of information which takes the metaphysical form of a past life. As we heal them, the experiences bring with them learnings, understandings and qualities and most of all the energy which benefits our clients in their lives today.

In RAPSI we treat past lives in the same way as we treat any other part of the energetic structure. We acknowledge it, engage with it, learn from it, find its hidden light and give it the opportunity to radiate through the person who has 'created' or 'found' it as part of their energetic system. Just as the energy might take the form of a colour or a walnut, so it might take the form of someone from a past life.

Often there are various people who have been involved in the crucial past life drama, and they all make themselves known. Our job is to acknowledge all of them, listen to all of them and understand that they were all acting the best way they knew how at the time and that they all come from and contain light. We then make sure that they understand this too. We ask them to explain and listen to one another – and eventually to forgive and be reconciled with one another, and release the protective layers which create all the pain and hurt and have kept the light trapped, possibly for centuries. We treat all players in a past life drama, and the environment, as being part of the person's larger multi-dimensional self. If you found it in your system, it's probably 'yours', and it's something you need to resolve if you want to regain its energy. In so doing, you may well also be healing people, events and possibly entire cultures and communities from the past.

93

Yes but ... *if I start engaging with past lives, isn't it going to take more than one lifetime to recover all the energy that has been hidden over centuries?*

No. Firstly, you don't necessarily deliberately engage with past lives. For some people, sometimes, they emerge. Others don't seem to meet them. The determining characteristic seems to be whether or not something has to be resolved and you are the vehicle for this healing and learning.

Secondly, from our experience there are usually one or two pivotal past lives which are influencing the present life, and they may have echoes in other past lives which then also show up for healing. It seems that a key piece of hidden energy keeps trying to bring itself to the attention of its 'host' through as many lifetimes as it takes for them to recognise it. Once it has been discovered, released and reintegrated, the work has been done for all lifetimes. Again, whether or not this is 'true' doesn't matter. What does matter is that our clients find missing parts of their energy which help them become whole.

Ancestral healing

Ancestral healing also involves past lives, but in this case the client is healing their direct ancestors, their bloodline going back through their mother or father or both.

Typically a person might find inside themselves a parent who exhibits the root cause of a problem that they are now dealing with. When they look inside or behind this parent, they discover a grandparent, and then that grandparent's parent, and so on back, all with the same hurt and the same cause, all needing healing. Most people believe that this happens in 'real life' (the sins of the fathers are visited on the sons, children abused by their parents become the abusers of their own children, victims become bullies), so it may well be that these patterns go back through the centuries.

Maybe a trait such as 'subservience' in women or 'coldness' on the part of the fathers shows up as the root cause of a problem manifesting in the current life. Having gone through the original doorway, the client finds a parent exhibiting the same problem and showing the root cause. The client can then summon those ancestors who need healing.

Sometimes one or two turn up, sometimes many more.

Placing them all in a line and then finding a doorway in the parent (or whoever is first in the line), the client looks through the doorway and right through the whole line of people to find the light at the back of the line. They ask that light to see light at the front of the line, in the present. We then ask the far light to come through, person by person, filling each with light until all the forms disappear and all that is left is the light in the present. This usually contains all the positive aspects of the family line, which brings the person support and a strong connection to their 'roots'.

It may be that a spokesperson for the ancestral line needs to be asked to self-select themselves to speak for their beliefs and their past actions and, ultimately, make peace with a person or people in their own time. That drama resolved, the light can then be brought through to the present time.

Occasionally, when healing some trait in the family (in the case of Sheila which follows, it was the father's guilt) an ancestral healing can draw in other souls/energetic beings who want healing. With Sheila, this involved those who died in the holocaust. We also have experience of a client healing millions who died in the famine in Biafra.

Sheila's story

Sheila, who had an important job in the business world, had shocked herself by having a bad car accident. Fortunately she was unhurt, she said, but she realised that part of her had not been focusing on driving and she had had other feelings which were distracting her.

'I don't know how to accept help', was one thing she said, 'I carry the bag for my father.' She marked out her solar plexus, and she meant that she carried a responsibility to succeed. His mother (her grandmother) died at her father's birth. His entire family was wiped out in the war and he carried guilt as a survivor, before himself dying young.

E Is your Dad still with you?

95

S *Yes.*

E *And his Mom?*

S *Yes.*

E *Say hello to your Dad and his Mom.*

S *Hello.*

E *How long have they been with you?*

S *Since he died.*

E *Did they ever make it to the light?*

S *No, he tried to find it but he felt earthbound because something was unfinished.*

E *What has he been doing?*

S *Watching me, enjoying my success.*

E *From where?*

S *From behind.* (She placed her hand on her solar plexus again, suggesting that it was the doorway to find them, or something else.)

The conversation continued and her dad was asked what he wanted for himself.

S/D *To bring the family to rest.*

E *Where are the family?*

S/D *Here with me.*

E *Do they want healing?*

S/D *Yes.*

E *Please have them come and be with you where we can see them.*

Sheila became visibly shocked and emotional.

S *Oh my God, they're all here.*

E *Who.*

S *My family, who died in the camps.* (In the holocaust.)

E *Who precisely?*

She named seven people, and while she had never seen photographs, she was able to name them because she 'felt' who they were. She wept as she spoke to each one and they smiled in recognition. When she was ready, she was asked to look into and through them (including Dad and Grandma) to find their light.

S *It's in their stomach.* (She touched her solar plexus indicating the shared 'doorway'.) *Hold on a moment, I can see some other people coming.*

E *Who are they?*

S *I don't know, but there are lots of them. Oh my God, they are from the camps.*

E *How many do you see?*

S *There are hundreds coming, literally hundreds. The place is opening up. I can see thousands.*

E *Speak to them. Thank them for coming and ask them why they have come to you.*

S *They were waiting, waiting to be healed, to be freed. They just followed my family. They saw the light.*

E *What light?*

S *My light.* (She burst into tears.)

It transpired that the distraction which she felt and which had contributed to her car accident was this part of her system not in her body which was a light shining like a beacon, waiting to be discovered. The healing which followed involved finding the light through and beyond the throng of people and finding the source of their being. Looking back through to the adult Sheila, that light saw the light in her and above her. The three lights saw each other and, having established that the one light would ultimately reside in her, the distant light was helped by Sheila to come forward, radiating through all the beings whose forms dissolved, including finally her family, including her father and grandmother. In the end all the light filled her and she sat in utter amazement and relief. She said, *'I was the vehicle for their healing and my father is now at peace.'* Our hope is that people will learn to heal themselves without needing to have an accident first!

It was at this point that she mentioned that she had sustained some whiplash in the accident, but that after this healing the pain had totally vanished.

So how was it possible that her ancestral line extended to a whole group (200,000 she estimated)? The best that we can understand was that she was holding her father in her energy system, whether created from her energy, his energy or both. Nested within him were his family and the environment in which they died, and the whole structure was revealed by opening the doorway in her and then his solar plexus. Whatever was happening, Sheila certainly felt, as did we, that she was involved in healing much suffering.

Karen's story

Karen had been healing various aspects of her personal life and had come to us to continue the journey. She started by taking stock of how much she had achieved.

K *I have updated my life from being a baby to age 37, but I cannot get to 39, me now. I am missing two years.*

She did the sums and deduced that it was her two-year-old self she needed to find. Looking into herself with her inner eyes, she discovered an accumulation of energy in the back of her head which spelt out the word 'therapy'. When she looked further, she saw herself in a therapy room feeling oppressed, aged two.

K/2 *I need God. I need to forgive myself for being a willing victim. I suffered to be close to my Mom.*

This was her Unconscious Equation (see page 55). It didn't sound much like the words of a two year old, but we worked with what it said and it turned out that the two year old was making pictures of a therapy room to help describe to the adult Karen that she started to suffer at the age of two in order to be acceptable to Mum who was also suffering. Even at that young age, she knew she needed help.

K/2 *It's embarrassing to admit that I have needs. I didn't know how to feel, to let feelings in.*

Karen's inner Mum (her 'real' mother had died some time before) enters the conversation and talks to the two-year-old Karen.

K/M *You don't have to see that silly therapist. Let's go and eat.*

K *The little girl wants a hug. She's walked into her mother's light. It's not as warm as she would like. Mother is crying now. The pain she endured separated her from God, from people. She couldn't love me – and her mother couldn't love her, and so on back through the ancestry.*

E *Call your maternal line to be present.*

She did, and we worked with the whole maternal line to heal their suffering. We went on to find God and reconcile Mum and God and bring God's light to the two year old, expanding it, and on through Karen and beyond.

Jim's story

This story involved healing a past life within a past life. Jim was in his late 40s and wanted greater success and a long-term relationship. He was having difficulty choosing the direction that his business needed to take and felt he couldn't move forward. He vacillated backwards and forwards. When someone is seeking an external relationship, one of the first things we are curious about is their relationship with themselves. Sometimes before there can be a union outside, there needs to be union inside of anything which might be in conflict – masculine/feminine, younger/older, inner/outer, etc.

A past life story opened up when he looked through the doorway of his heart (which he had been pointing towards).

J   *There's a man weeping over his dead love. She died in his arms, from some sort of consumption. He feels his life is over. He cannot go on.*

(Note the language. He cannot go on, and Jim is having difficulty in moving forwards.)

We continued to gather information, talked to the two energies and began the process of finding light to heal both the man and his love. His light is inside him, but hers seems to be in front of her.

E   *Look into her light and follow it to source.*

J   *It has gone forward 400 years. She has reincarnated again as a woman. She has the memory of a great love, she cannot settle in a relationship, she goes backwards and forwards about whether to marry or not. She does not feel that she can commit to anyone through time.*

(Now we have elements which are contributing to Jim's lack of commitment and a 400-year gap providing the backwards and forwards pull that he feels.)

Jim transported her back to the first life, the couple were healed, their forms dissolved into light and the energy came forward, dissolving the form of the life 400 years later, and Jim was the recipient of all the light. Needless to say, this freed him to restructure his business and to begin a long-term relationship. This was the first time we had found a person's masculine and feminine energies spread over two lifetimes like this, with the need to heal a past life of a character who was herself, for Jim, a past life.

Jason's story

A past life was involved in healing 'the face of evil'. Jason was not a pretty sight. This was not a man opne found easy to hug, and everything in his life reflected back to him the fact that he was ugly on the outside and also ugly on the inside. He had even been an ugly screaming baby.

Session by session, as trust built, he would do little pieces of work, mostly to do with this lifetime. He cleared his mother, who was a drug addict, his unknown father (who appeared to him during a session), the foster parents who had been cruel to him, the care home supervisor who had sexually assaulted him, the prison staff and on, and on.

In one session, tracing his feelings of rage, which we had not been able to resolve fully, he found a door. It was made of heavy wood, arched and studded with metal bands and a heavy ring for a handle. Opening it, he found himself in a dungeon and saw a prisoner being tortured. It was the time of the Inquisition. The man was falsely accused and the healing involved the prisoner, his torturers, his accusers and the church. As Jason healed each participant in this drama, his face began to change, his leer began to melt, the frown on his forehead dissolved, his right eye which was recessed more than the left came forward, and his right ear which was forward of the left moved back. It was truly amazing. He was quite handsome, and he went to look at himself in the mirror and came back stunned and grinning. He had blossomed from the inside and reversed the physical transformation that his life experience had dealt him.

Jason is not unique. We have had other clients who sense that they came into this life with past life experiences of having been tortured. A woman who became involved in sado-masochism had been tortured as a 'witch' in a past life; a past life little girl who was beaten and locked up by her Victorian teacher and who died in terror had shown up as a vindictive schoolteacher in this life, etc. We stress again that not everyone needs to resolve past life or ancestral connections, but when they do, a whole range of unexplained feelings and symptoms – and even physical characteristics – can be improved.

Horatio/Gordon's story

Horatio was born with a 'poncy' name, not one that that he felt comfortable with, so at the earliest opportunity, he changed it. Alienated from his family, he changed his last name also – something he reversed when he discovered that his father was disinheriting him! But he kept his new first name, Gordon. However, he never felt happy as Gordon either and increasingly he felt that he was in the wrong body. He went in for body piercing but nothing he did seemed to help him feel comfortable. He had discovered as a teenager that he was gay, and increasingly he felt that his natural gender was to be a woman and he set about researching the procedure involved in having a sex-change.

This is not a quick procedure and engaging in counselling was part of the process – which was when we met him. To his surprise, Gordon discovered that his feelings of discomfort, his strong feelings of femininity and his urge to change gender were coming from a past life as a high-born aristocratic lady from the 1700s. One irony was that the name of her great love, a military man killed in action, was Horatio!

Life can truly be stranger than fiction! Gordon's desire to change his gender began to evaporate when the energy of the aristocratic lady was integrated.

When people say things like 'I don't feel as if I'm in the right body' or are clearly concerned about their sexuality or comfort as a particular gender, it is possible that there may be past life influences. Another RAPSI explanation might be that the feeling comes from a person's masculine or feminine energy being suppressed in this lifetime due to the environment, for example, a bullying father or suffocating mother.

Chapter Thirteen

Spirit attachments

There are occasions when the energy form that is discovered within or around a person does not present itself as a past life of the client or as a part of the client. It may say that it attached itself to the person of today, often to learn, to get attention, to maintain a connection with life and/or the living, sometimes causing mischief or distress. For this to have happened, there has to be something needing clearing in the client, a reason why they attracted the spirit in the first place, so there will always be a mutual healing needed. Sometimes the 'attached spirit' does not know that it is dead and sometimes it presents itself as something alien, or unpleasant, or cloaked in darkness.

The subject of spirit attachment and how one works with attached spirits is gaining credibility in various circles around the western world. Of course this is nothing new in the world of indigenous tribes or to some eastern belief systems. 75 per cent of the world believes in existence beyond death as well as reincarnation. The possible explanation for spirit attachment is that energy, ejected from a body at the moment of a violent death and not knowing the body has died, finds itself in limbo. Somehow it communicates with the person of today, who is also fragmented. It has been only the western world which rejected the idea, but more and more people are beginning to give it credence again.

Psychiatrists in the UK, for example, are beginning to take notice of 'the spirit world' and there is a thriving section on Psychiatry and Spirituality within The Royal College of Psychiatrists. There is also a growing interest in the idea that some apparent mental illness may have their origins in the realm of spirit and need to be addressed other than by drugs. The Spirit Release Foundation in the UK was created in 1999 and has begun to give trainings and make itself and its ideas known. (Eileen and Clive have been part of this group from its inception.)

What RAPSI offers to the subject of spirit release is the understanding of source light hidden within 'dark forces', which is typically unknown to the so-called dark force itself, to the client and often to the practitioner. We feel that it is of the utmost importance for practitioners to understand this. In the past, the healing process entailed the 'dark force' being persuaded or coerced into 'going to the light' to achieve cleansing, 'bad' becoming 'good'. This is not what RAPSI is teaching.

Firstly, we agree that there are energies, spirits, which need healing, and some may indeed present themselves as a spirit attachment. It is how one views them, how one approaches them that is important.

Secondly, there is no dispute that these attachments can cause pain, suffering, fear, sometimes ill health, etc. The results can be quite disturbing, negative, and can feel very malevolent. What is vital is to understand that the cause of the malevolence is the absence of light and our job is to wake up these entities to their true nature, their true energetic inheritance. More than once, we have been close to tears when working with such an entity, which has been engaging in despicable thoughts or activities. As we took it inside itself, lo and behold, it discovered the light. Can you imagine thinking that you are the scum of the earth only to find that you are part of the divine source and that you hold that within you? That your very negativity came from your disengagement from that light? And furthermore that disengagement was not only purposeful but was the light's way of protecting itself? At that point we have seen the biggest, toughest, nastiest entities melt into tears of understanding and relief.

So we will work with a spirit attachment in much the same way as we work with any energetic form. The basic difference is the final freed and expanded light, typically, does not radiate through the client's body but returns to the light. We do, however, always give it and the client the choice.

Through this process of healing the spirit attachment, the client moves from feeling disempowered and under the control of something else, to being able to assist in the healing and take charge of their own inner space.

One bonus of working in this way is that we are able to work with people who died with important issues left unresolved – both issues which relate directly to them which are affecting our client, and issues between the different people who were involved in the drama. Of course, if they have turned up in our client's energetic structure, then they are all relevant and need to be resolved.

We have also been asked whether we 'believe' in aliens and abductions. To date, working with extraterrestrials has been rare for us, but we have encountered such experiences in two clients, in other people's workshops and with a healer in Israel. We don't believe or disbelieve. We work from within the person's energetic structure with whatever form the energy takes. Whether the energy takes the form of an alien, a past life, a younger self or the spirit/s of the dead, we work to find their positive intention, educate it about its situation, and then find and release the light at its centre so that it may radiate.

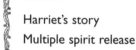

Harriet's story
Multiple spirit release

'Anyone who has ever suffered from depression will understand its effect on your peace of mind. It is a dark and painful experience. As for its reason, those trusted few people who may have been privy to your feelings could never understand why a person with so many opportunities in life could be so grim about themselves.'
These were Harriet's words.

In July 1999, Eileen received a call from Harriet sounding weak and very fragile: *'I am having a bad time. I overdosed last week.'* She said that Social Services were sending someone to visit her, but that she wanted an appointment with Eileen. This is the account Eileen wrote of the sessions.

Initial session 2 August 1999 (one hour) Harriet is a professional-looking, nicely dressed young woman of 31. She is clearly feeling very low and depressed, and is almost totally negatively focused. *'I don't like me or my life. I want to go to a different existence, a nicer one. I don't have faith in myself. I let people choose me. I will sleep with anyone. I don't want to be here anymore.'*

(I wonder 'who', which consciousness, is actually doing the talking here.)

During this session, I learn that she feels almost totally disempowered. *'I don't choose and I feel at the mercy of the world around me.'* I find that she is particularly judgemental about her parents and calls them *'selfish, unthinking, ignorant, unwise and thoughtless'.*

As I gather information from Harriet, it isn't long before we find ourselves back at her beginnings, where it is revealed that her mother had had to cope with crisis after crisis as she carried Harriet. As a result, the decision Harriet made as a foetus was: *'I am not happy and I can't be happy again. I can't see a way out of this.'* This was the start of her depression.

As the session continues, I help her to clarify a positive aim for herself and her therapy sessions. She starts with a desire to *'value myself and be assertive'.* Then she realises that, in addition to judging her parents, she judges herself severely, which leaves her feeling demeaned and prevents her from feeling positive. We further learn through our questioning that when she was about three years old her grandfather had abused her older sister. Becoming aware of this revelation seems to give her some relief.

Harriet reveals that her method of coping ever since she was a foetus had been to fragment her energetic being. Some of her energy was cut off, compressed, suppressed. Some of it was ejected entirely out of her body which, she argued, was a good thing as it enabled her to seek, find, recover and reintegrate her split-off energy. *'My creative side is up there.'* (As she says this, she is gesturing upwards and towards the right, away from herself.) *'I was crushed – disconnected from Mum. Mum creates a vortex. Some of my energy is outside; some is inside.'* (Splitting energy creates a vacuum which can attract other energy.)

Harriet's goal then becomes *'to not be negative – to know that, when I am unhappy, there is light at the end of the tunnel'.* (Note her choice of words.) At the end of the session, she says, *'I want to be happy, fully relaxed, whole'.*

I ask her how close she feels she is to her goal on a scale of 1 to 10. She says she began the session with 4 out of 10 and now feels at 6, but is aiming for 10. I ask how many sessions she thinks she will need to reach 10. She prophetically declares 'three'. (She is already allowing her positive instincts to speak.)

Second session 10 August 1999 (90 minutes) I begin by asking Harriet how she has been feeling since the initial session. She has been feeling tired and is suffering from her usual hay fever and chronic eczema. *'However,'* she says, *'I think of myself more positively. I feel more relaxed and more secure, more solid, more grown-up and independent'.* We do another 1 to 10 scoring check and she decides she feels at 7.

As we get back into the depths of her memories, she begins to recall an episode that took place when she was three – the murder of her Aunt Maureen and her aunt's three-year-old daughter, Harriet's cousin, Joan. It hadn't made much of an impact, as far as she remembers, as she had been too young to appreciate what was going on, but as she speaks, she begins to become aware of feelings of guilt – guilt that she is alive – and wonders whether they are jealous. *'I'm here and they're not. I want to get away from that shadow of death that has grown, as I have got older. I was always a melancholy child.'*

Harriet explains that, in recent years, she has thought more and more frequently of her aunt and cousin, but did not understand why this was happening. I then ask Harriet to look into herself (literally) and she finds, much to her amazement, that her aunt and cousin are within the left hemisphere of her brain. I had noticed her signalling in that direction as she spoke about them and suspected the presence there of a 'doorway'. I helped Harriet to initiate a conversation with them and also made direct contact with them myself. Maureen tells Harriet that they were there *'to make her aware of what had happened to them and to get some completion'.* At this point, Harriet's new goal becomes *'to make peace with Auntie and Cousin Joan, to help them be at peace, and to feel less guilty for being here'.*

Aunt Maureen (through Harriet) tells the tragic story of her thwarted love. She and Khalid had been very much in love, but his parents were completely against the union as she, Maureen, was not of their culture. Khalid was going to marry Maureen anyway. Khalid's mother, Zara, unable to bear the thought of this, had murdered both Maureen and little Joan by choking them to death while her husband stood guard. (They were both later imprisoned for the murders and died in prison.)

Further exploration of Harriet's internal universe and various 'doorways' uncovers the presence of Zara and her husband, both of whom have been residing in Harriet's right cerebral hemisphere. It becomes clear that these spirits need to 'complete' something to be at peace, and that they are the source of Harriet's negative feelings. On occasion, it is their words that she has been speaking.

Khalid, who had committed suicide after the murder, is found outside Harriet's body, in front of her and slightly to the right. He adamantly refuses to connect with, talk to or forgive his parents. However, Maureen is willing to forgive Zara and tells her: *I really loved your son. It was such a waste*'. Maureen then says to Harriet: *We know that we've caused you pain. We stayed as a link to meet them (Khalid and his parents) and to say what needed saying*'.

Khalid finally speaks and says: *I'm putting an end to this. I find it difficult to forgive. We would have had everything. It's appalling – the horror of it, the ugliness of it. It's just beyond my comprehension*'. His mother Zara then responds: *I am disgusted with myself. I should never have done something like this and dragged my husband into it as well*'.

Khalid's father has remained silent, as has little Joan, but the links have been made and everyone is given the opportunity to say whatever he or she needs or wants to say. We talk about the unfortunate cultural barriers and the misfortunes – like this one – that can arise because of them. Then, I get the sense that I must have Khalid's parents call their community together to both teach and heal them all. Harriet reports that hundreds of people are gathering as she continues to look into her right brain area. I suggest that a spokesperson be chosen from among them. We remind them all of the tragedy that has occurred and the spokesperson says: *We are all ashamed. We all think it was such a waste*'. Finally, Khalid is able to address his parents and tell them: *I forgive you, Mother and Father*'. *We love our son, we always have,*' replies his mother.

Aunt Maureen then says: *I'm glad it's been resolved, so that I can stop thinking about not being here and at the same time being here, growing up with Harriet*'. When I ask her what her next evolutionary step is, she answers: *To regenerate, to go out [come out of Harriet] to say goodbye*'. We discuss whether her and Joan's energies will recycle and integrate into Harriet to help her realise the benefits of expression and manifestation. Joan then speaks for the first time, saying that she *wants to go to the Light*'. Her grandparents come for her. *Say hello to Maureen for us,*' they say. *We think of her, and we want to thank Harriet.*' *Goodbye,*' says Harriet.

And the other forms? They, too, want to be released and recycled

107

into the present Harriet. I ask her to look inside them (using the 'x-ray vision' of her inner eyes) to find their light, and help it to radiate through their metaphysical bodies to release them into pure light, which Harriet then senses expanding within her own body. *'How do you feel now?'* I ask her. She replies, *'Shell-shocked! Brilliant! It's just going to be me now.'*

Third and final session 8 September 1999 (one hour) I ask Harriet how she's been. She is clearly feeling better – more positive and confident. She reports that she has given a presentation in front of a large group at work, and surprised herself by feeling good about it and doing well. She feels she no longer needs self-assertiveness training. Her eczema is clearing.

We spend this final hour dealing with her obsessive desire to work and to over-achieve which, in the past, had been the major way that she could feel good about herself. We deal with the dialogues in her head to allow her more creativity, a process that had begun since her second session. She has bought herself a piano. *'I will learn to play it,'* she tells me. *'I'm going to finish decorating my room, and I'll buy a sewing machine. I look forward to being more creative at work. Before this evening, I couldn't see any scope for it, but now I can.'*

A follow-up phone call 8 November 2000 Fourteen months have passed. I am calling Harriet to ask for permission to write up and publish the work we did together as well as to see how she is doing. She is delighted to hear from me and says that she has just qualified as a solicitor. *'Things are really hectic at work, but I am settled.'* Faxing over a summary of the long-term results of her healing work, she adds: *'Every year or so, I used to suffer a crisis of confidence that became increasingly more severe over the years and, from an early age, I began to consider the option of death. But my position now is that, no matter how tough things get, that particular notion is no longer an option. I have also found, since receiving help from Eileen, that, although I still have lows which can be painful, I consider that the source is my being sensitive, rather than depressive. I now have the ability to cope. Indeed, as my belief in myself has grown, I have found that I can actually cope with quite a lot.*

'To summarise, I now have what I never had before – a personal sense of proportion and perspective, essential tools for a happy mind and life.'

Harriet's story was first published in the BASR (now Spirit Release Foundation) Newsletter, Winter 2000.

Chapter Fourteen

Absent healing

If thought forms are energy which can have a profound effect on one's own physical self, there is increasing evidence that thoughts can affect others – people, animals and plants. Energy affects energy, and distance seems to be no barrier.

In some models of 'absent healing' (healing someone who is not present), the healer may be taught to send their energy to another person to help alleviate their pain. They may work with the person's unconscious mind or they may be taught to draw in divine energy and act as a conduit, sending the energy via their focused intention. Or they are taught to increase their energetic vibration and, in turn, help a patient increase the rate of their own energetic vibration (sometimes working with symbols) to help the body heal itself. There is sometimes a belief that when they activate their healing of others they may be making themselves vulnerable and taking in 'negative energies' and so there are rituals to cleanse the body or to cloak the body in light.

For us, it is radiating light from the inside out that symbolises and demonstrates a healthy human system and is the key to health for the facilitator and the client alike. Those that have achieved this say that their energy field dissolves or dispels any negativity that might previously have affected them, so cleansing rituals for the healer are not necessary in the same way. For someone who is unwell, the best way to help them to heal themselves is to help them find and expand their pockets of energy until they are fully radiating. This can be done face-to-face or at a distance, with their knowledge or without. We do not aim to put light or energy in, we aim to help draw it out.

Think of a worried parent sending 'worry' and their negatively-tinged energy to their child. Does it help? We suggest not. Instead, we teach the parent to see their child in their mind's eye and find their compressed or hidden energy, their innermost essence. Then, by looking in, and yet further in, thanking each layer they meet, until they find the pure white light, and then seeing that light expanding and radiating through the child's body.

Typically both the parent and the youngster may notice the effects. Since what the parent is seeing may be formed out of their own energy, this healing is transforming something that is unwell, unhappy and may be 'misbehaving' in themselves. Often it is the parent who needs to do some work. After the healing, the parent's connection to their child shifts and often the child's behaviour changes appropriately. The parent feels relief, trust and peace and this alone can positively affect the relationship and the situation.

We hold a healing circle monthly with a few of our graduates meeting together and others tapping in remotely. The focus can be the living or the deceased, an individual, family, statesman or a culture, anyone who is suggested or who asks for help. In our experience, the process of absent healing works although it is difficult sometimes to verify this, especially if you are healing the departed. Even if the only benefit is to help the 'healer' feel better about someone else's plight, that has to be an advantage. However, for us, there is more happening. The healers certainly feel better for the experience – many report feeling the healing energy flowing through themselves. It seems you cannot heal others without also healing yourself. And we have also received comments from people at great distances saying that they did notice a positive improvement in their condition at the time of the healing.

Most of the examples we know about were done by us or trainees on our courses.

Sophie's Dad's healing

Sophie was first introduced to absent healing on a one-day RAPSI course with Clive and Eileen and has done it a couple of times on friends she knew were in distress, but with no confirmation of whether or not it had worked. However recently her father was suffering with a prostate infection. When he'd had it on a previous occasion, it had proved very difficult to shift and he'd felt very ill over a period of months. On this occasion, Sophie tried absent healing.

She telepathically scanned his body and, after obtaining his permission to proceed (also telepathically)*, found a small brown 'walnut' in the centre of his chest. After saying hello and thanking it for whatever job it was doing, she looked inside and it immediately burst open and large quantities of black 'pus' poured out. Although her immediate reaction was one of disgust, she remembered that this was just an energetic layer, and thanked it for doing its job. As soon as she did that, she understood that this black mess was all the difficult experiences her father had had in his life (and he'd had quite a few), and they were locked up inside so that he could continue to show a cheerful face to the world. Knowing that black is very often a major cover of the light, Sophie looked inside the black and found pure white light which immediately started streaming out. She continued to see the white light radiating throughout his body and beyond and felt very positive about he experience. The next day he was well enough to get up and later that day got some antibiotics which cleared up the infection. He normally has an adverse reaction to antibiotics, but on this occasion he remained well and cheerful throughout and the infection cleared up. Sophie felt good too.

Ellen's healing

A group of trainees in 2002 undertook the absent healing of one of their number who could not be there that day. The trainees located at least five doorways between them: head and down the back (cloak over head, back and halfway down on the left, left back and bottom of head), throat, heart and solar plexus/stomach. Afterwards they compared how they felt about the activity:

- *It seemed easier to explore someone else rather than myself.*
- *This seemed to be affecting me and I wondered if this was actually about me not her. I notice my sceptical self judging the process.*
- *I practise Reiki and I felt a 'yoyo' sensation, felt faint and wanted to cry.*
- *Using visualisation is still a stopper for me.*
- *When I explored her throat, I felt sick.*

* In our experience, all beings are grateful for the chance to be healed.

- *When I looked into her head, I saw purple, a dark centre, a vortex and then a foetus and felt sick. The foetus was helping Ellen see or not see.*
- *I saw a pulsing light, flashing, a golden rim, then calmer black, dark, velvety dark, comfortable.*

Since we are all connected, we may well be drawn to areas where we also have work to do and likewise when we do work on ourselves, or on a client, it can positively affect another person in our/their lives. As you develop your sensitivity you will also notice that you can feel some of the experience of the client, and that this is different to your normal experience of being, and by using the feelings, the knowing, this can guide your work with the client. Ellen said she was pleased to have been useful, even at a distance. She felt it clearly did her some good and she rejoined the group the next day.

Monet's healing

We (Clive and Eileen) went to see the magnificent Monet collection in London. As we walked around, we came to one particular picture which was open and full of light. Moving on we saw the pictures becoming darker and more compact, until they were the truly dense large room-size paintings of his famous lilies. From the light-filled picture onwards, we both noticed independently that our hearts were aching. Sitting down to have some lunch, we decided to contact Monet and find out what the pain was to do with and to give him an absent healing. As you do!

The process in this case was for Clive to close his eyes and to be in himself while Eileen asked the questions and guided the facilitation. Pretty quickly Clive sensed a presence, which he described as feeling able to know things, sense things and say things as the other person while losing no sense of personal identity. Others have called this aspect of what we do mediumship or a Shamanic process. We just do it. Much to our surprise, the person that Clive was able to 'talk' to was Monet's grandson. When we explained that we had felt our hearts ache, he told us that Monet had suffered a heart attack and that there was a period when he changed his painting style and experimented with that increasing light, which mirrored happiness in his personal life. His agent told him that the pictures would not sell, so he returned to his earlier style but became increasingly sombre. Listening to this at the energetic level, we could imagine Monet's light breaking through briefly and then being capped – with the subsequent pressure creating heart problems. Thanking the grandson, we called Monet and gave him a healing for which he thanked us. Checking with the exhibition materials, we found the information about Monet to be accurate.

We don't always get involved in healing deceased and famous people (although that was not an isolated incident), but we do think that it is possible to heal the energy of people who have died. Death does not seem to be any barrier to healing.

Sarah's Dad's healing

We, Eileen and Clive, were in Israel to see Eileen's Mom into her new retirement home. We were talking to Sarah, the sweet lady who was helping with the paperwork. Eileen was talking about her Dad's death in late 2001, and Sarah's eyes become moist. She talked about losing her own father at a relatively young age, when he was in his 50s. With her permission, later that day we did an absent healing. Sarah had shown us a picture of her father, so his image came easily and after introductions he started to speak about his life, his pride for Sarah, showing her in a blue outfit as a young teenager, of his relationship with his family and of his time as an officer fighting in the Sinai and being desperately upset about the death of his men and others and the war in general. There was more, including favourite sayings and phrases he used. The next day we told a somewhat incredulous Sarah what had happened. She moved from a natural scepticism to attentiveness when she recognised the blue outfit (her school uniform) and some of the phrases which were only known to her or her family.

Raymond's healing

The familiar phrase and tone of voice was also a confirmation in the contacting of Raymond, a jazz musician, shortly after his death. Clive and Eileen had sensed Raymond's energy at his funeral and then spoken to him at home. They told his widow Florence about this and she went to their home.

Clive experienced Raymond above him and Raymond was able to look down and describe what he saw. Coming down, Clive felt him approach him from behind and then Clive was able to speak for him. Hearing Clive speaking with Raymond's native accent and using a nickname that only Florence knew was deeply satisfying to Florence as he spoke to her through Clive. She said she knew his energy was still around. At different points, Clive felt himself crying Raymond's tears. This was clearly not a case of integrating energy in Florence and it was Raymond who was given the healing and comfort.

Lesley's Mum and Dad's healing

It is normal for clients to discover inner parents and they are usually crafted out of the person's own energy doing some kind of job, protective or otherwise but always positively intended. This is how the conversation went:

E *Your parents are departed?*

L *Yes.*

E *Do they still exist in or around you?*

L *Yes.*

E *Do they bring a set of beliefs?*

L *Yes.*

E *Enhancing or limiting?*

L *Limiting.*

E *Do they have a good relationship with each other? Is it a positive one?*

L *Not positive. Conflict and struggle.*

We then got Lesley to talk to them and it transpired that they had been with her from an early age. Unconsciously Lesley had put them there to try and work out how to please them both, and failing to please either as they could not be pleased. Pleasing others at the expense of herself was a problem in her life.

L *I want to be strong enough to risk being my vulnerable, sensitive,
delicate side without being trampled on. I want to be able to risk it. I
want to be free of this mental clutter which holds 'me' down.*

(Note the language. 'Being held down' suggests something 'up' which
needs to come down and integrate.)

E *How do you feel, compared to them?*

L *Very childlike and vulnerable.*

E *Are they big or small as you look at them?*

L *Fairly big. Scary. They are in space.*

E *Did they know that you are scared of them?*

L *No.*

E *Do they know now?*

L *Yes.*

E *Are they in a dark or light space?*

L *Light space.*

Lesley begins yawning and we find that the air where her parents are
is rarefied with little oxygen – she is feeling their feelings in their
situation. They are on a plateau on a mountain with a younger Lesley
who floated off when life became too difficult to bear. Lesley knows
that she wants them down off the mountain, and with the help of a
'controller' in her (which she had found in her head just before
finding her parents' energy), she begins the process of bringing them
down.

E *Controller, did you know they were on this mountain?*

L/C *I did not know it was a mountain. I did know that she was up there,
but I didn't know how to help her.*

E *Is it OK to rescue her?*

L/C *Yes.*

E *What do you see?*

We want to get information and awaken everything from all
perspectives.

L/C *The little one with an angelic presence, big, white and huge.*

E *A he or a she or neither?*

L/C *A she.*

E *Mom and Dad, looking at the controller in her head, what do you see?*

L/M&D *Big bright eyes.*

The session continues, involving discussion with all the elements, including the angelic being. Lesley continues to yawn for oxygen. The parents have been doing the job of being critical of Lesley, one in each ear. Shit in stereo! Eventually the angel brings little Lesley down to sit in her lap and big Lesley stops yawning. After healing the parents and saying a fond farewell, something she thought she would never be able to do, the angel takes the parents into itself, light becoming more light. Their forms disappear and the light fills the child who is then absorbed into Lesley as light, filling her with energy and softness.

This was another style of absent healing, this time healing deceased parents whose forms were held earthbound, and dissolved back into light, while at the same time recovering the client's out-of-body self. Lesley's nested energy was released, expanded and freed to radiate .

The healing that follows is a report from a trainee on a weekend course.

Pamela's healing

This is the account of a healing given by a trainee on the second weekend of our nine-month RAPSI training course for Pamela who was absent because of illness. It is in the words of one of the trainees.

The end of another fascinating but tiring day – supporting people is hard work. Eileen proposes that we absent-heal Pamela – one of our group who's recovering from viral meningitis. The others are keen. The sceptical Yorkshire woman in me is thinking, 'Oh please. She's 60 miles away recovering anyway and nothing I can do will make a jot of difference, besides which it's already past 6 pm, I've had enough and I'm impatient to go.' I agree reluctantly.

Having sought permission of her unconscious for the healing, we visualise Pamela, which I do with difficulty, and then 'see' the light in her radiating. I do as I'm told with no expectation of success.

To my amazement, as I see the light expand through her, in my mind's eye, it radiates to me in an almost tangible way, then back to her and from her to me, back and forth unendingly. It feels terrific, like breast-feeding only less tiring. Two people intimately rhythmically connected. I share this with the rest of the group feeling terribly pleased with myself, and daring to hope that one day I might indeed become a healer of sorts. When I get home, I suddenly realise I'm feeling very happy. When I ask myself why, the answer comes loud and clear: healing Pamela also healed me.

Yes but ... *isn't it wrong to heal others without their permission?*

Healing in the RAPSI model means discovering light that is trapped and that needs and wants freeing. As a polite opening, we will ask permission of the person telepathically, but we have never encountered a system which did not want to be healed. Why would it? On the very rare occasions that we know of other people encountering possible resistance, we have encouraged them to discuss with the energy why it doesn't want healing, and almost always the real reason is because of resistance in the 'healer' who is coming from a fear-based model or the 'no' is simply the first protective answer. The best protection for all of us is to be fully radiating ourselves – and we would never deliberately withhold healing from others. Our mission is to help as many people as possible, alive or dead, come to wholeness.

One last thing to say. We do not always know consciously whether absent healing has worked or not, but we still think it's worth doing. However we do not always expect that a person bounces back to full health immediately or perhaps ever. If that person has reached the end of their natural life, then it might be appropriate that they die. We would still offer healing, but in the knowledge that what we are doing is helping them resolve an energetic holding pattern so that they can die 'well' when they need to.

Chapter Fifteen

The language of dis-ease

Each person's story and journey to health and well being is unique to them and it would be foolish and irresponsible to extrapolate that one specific illness is always the result of a particular set of circumstances, or experiences and apply that across the board.

However, our experience is that an energetic origin has been discovered in all the instances of chronic and less serious physical (and emotional and mental) symptoms that we have worked with over the years, which suggests that the idea of 'dis-ease', stemming from fragmentation of the consciousness/soul or spirit is the starting point. Changing this energetic pattern of fragmentation can positively affect a symptom. Further research is needed to discover whether these patterns contribute to or even lead to all physical and organic breakdown or abnormality.

Scientific research is beginning to provide the proof that this might be so. We speak from our own experience and we look forward to the day when science proves beyond a doubt the effect of the energetic realm on the physical.

It would also seem to be possible that the AIDS epidemic in Africa, for example, could come from a group consciousness or a cultural consciousness which has shared issues which need healing. Harriet's story (page 104) is one example from many which involved healing a whole culture whose 'laws' led to death, in this case by murder.

We have noticed that certain illnesses seem to be linked with other 'personality' symptoms, and this is frequently indicated by language used by the client (see literal listening, page 42). In some of the cases quoted below we may have only worked with a client briefly, so we were not able to see them through to full wholeness, which in its entirety can take some time. In some cases, we have worked with people where we have not been able to help in terms of physical recovery but they have been able to move on in life or to pass on from life with some relief. Perhaps that was the importance of the work we did.

The main point is that we are not in a fight against disease. That is old language belonging to an old paradigm. We are interested in curing, healing, transforming. Rather than working with disease, we work with the person and their energetic structure in their quest for wholeness.

What we noticed particularly in these next cases was how people's inner decisions and intentions could affect their physical well-being.

Rosemary's story

Multiple Sclerosis *'My mother and father separated. He kidnapped me once and when my mother got me back, we began to move. Every few months, we moved address, changing schools, changing friends. One day, I said to myself 'I want to stop moving.'*
Rosemary's request was granted and she gradually began to *stop moving* as her MS developed. In our sessions, we found the 'I', the 'masculine energy' in Rosemary's left brain hemisphere, that took the decision, and the 'myself' who collaborated, aged five, in her spine. We traced the deterioration in her physical structure to her early 20s. After we had released and united the different energies, the deterioration slowed and even though Rosemary was still confined to a wheelchair, she found purpose in her life and became a healer/therapist herself. We wonder what effect we might have been able to have had we met Rosemary some years earlier.

Philip's story

ME (Myalgic Encephalomyelitis) *My parents are very successful academics, and at school I shone at everything. However, as I got into my teens, it became harder and harder to keep up the standards I set myself. When I got to university, I just couldn't go on, I seemed to have lost myself and I got ME. I was exhausted.'*
The 'I', which Philip found in his left brain hemisphere, was exhausted.

The 11 year old was there with his parents whom he was pleasing by passing exams. Philip found 'ME' (himself) in two places, in his right brain hemisphere and in his stomach. 'Me' was lost and had been missing since the age of three when his creativity, his expressiveness, was squashed with the help of his parents' attitudes and their inability to receive and value his bubbling energy and its expression. 'Play' was not valued, 'Study, reading and sums' were valued. 'Me/Myself' was mothballed. Gradually losing steam, 'I' continued to strive until he no longer could, his energy spent. ME, the disease, struck signalling the search for 'Me'. 'Me/Myself' provided the doorway to a wellspring of energy and when it was united with the energy of 'I' and of the present Philip, a new balanced life was created. Philip went back to university, completed his degree and learned to play jazz guitar!

When you think of his case of ME, just imagine an 'elastic band' with a three year old at one end and a young adult and his 11-year-old driver stretching the rubber band until it will stretch no more. Either the band breaks or one has to go back to collect the three year old's energy. Is ME, the disease, always a search for 'me', the self?

Julian's story

Eczema *'I keep everyone away.'*
As a workshop participant, Julian was asked to draw an energy map by scanning his body using his 'inner eyes' (see Body Scanning and Energy Mapping on page 40). He drew a red line all round his body, which was the eczema he had suffered from for 18 years. As he said, *'It keeps everyone away'.* Part of his work with us involved understanding why 'suffering' was important to him. The energetic red line responded to his questioning and explained that it was compressed energy keeping out his mother's energy (feeling anxious) and which his energetic awareness had detected in the womb. Unconsciously, he had formed an extra 'skin', not allowing his own skin to breathe easily. His Unconscious Equation (see page 55) was that suffering (with eczema) provided him with a sense of selfhood, with an identity.

Looking through the energetic layer of red, then yellow, he found Light ('cool white light'). As he freed that Light and then brought in more light, which had been kept on the outside (he was keeping part of himself out there), we all watched with amazement as Julian's skin became very red and then cooled and became supple and moist. Over the next 20 minutes the signs of eczema faded away. Six months later we got in touch with him and learnt his eczema had never returned. The eczema had been a 'healthy' allergic reaction to being smothered by his mother's feelings of anxiety. It was a survival mechanism, kept in place by an unconscious decision that suffering (with eczema) was part of his freedom and self-identity. One can see the irony: 'freedom' on the outside, but trapped on the inside.

Grace's story

Stomach cancer *'My body is not important, I am more than my body.'* Grace was ill with a cancerous growth. Over a two-month period, she came for sessions and discovered the little child who had learned in the family that she wasn't important. Once she released this energy into the present, her condition improved. Then she stopped coming and in a home visit, she let slip that everyday she chanted, *'My body is not important, I am more than my body'*. As part of her ritual, she focused on rising out of her body (so as not to feel bodily discomfort) to a place above her head. After meditating there, she returned to her body. She did not know that that place above her head was a doorway to vast amounts of energy and light for self-healing and that it needed to be drawn in. What she did realise, too late, was that her relationship with this place was of 'one up' and 'one down'. She had attributed all the importance to the 'higher self' and no importance to her body. Unfortunately, she was beyond being able to do our work, so we simply were with her. She died not long afterwards. Contrast this with Lacey's story.

Lacey's story

Ovarian cancer *'I know that I can beat this, I won't let it get me down.'* Lacey had developed a sizeable ovarian tumour. We found 'I' who was in the back of Lacey's head, a five year old who was angry about moving from the country of her birth. As an adult she would always 'drive myself'. 'Up' above her head we found 'Me', a 'higher self'.

(Remember that 'higher' simply refers to location and not to any superiority, although this self was indeed behaving as if it was superior.) The higher self thought that it was helping by criticising her. Its intent was to guide her from on high. In the ovary was 'It', 'a baby', that could not get love or milk from its mother. Boy was it angry! Just imagine the energetic bile brewing in the ovary! The higher self part of Lacey needed some convincing that it was better to come down into its 'vehicle' which it deemed 'a mess', and Lacey was wedded to the idea that she needed to keep the energy up there, as it gave her better 'in'-'sights' 'into' 'the world' (listen to the language). This was a system in conflict. When the energy was released from the metaphysical ovary, and enabled to expand, and the energy from behind the head came down and joined it in the body, her physical appearance lightened, and the light above came down and began to radiate through and expanded beyond the skin line. This was the last time we saw Lacey. She did not need the operation, since the tumour had mysteriously shrunk back to the size of a small cyst which she then worked on homoeopathically.

Maxime's story

Pre-cancerous throat condition *'It feels like something is stuck in my throat stopping me speaking out.'*
Maxime has a pre-cancerous throat condition. Looking into her throat, she discovered her 'mother' when Maxime was a child. Her mother is deeply religious believing that 'suffering' is a natural part of living and is strongly wedded to her faith and to the advice of her church and its minister. A mother of several children, she had little time for Maxime, and little Maxime had 'swallowed her words' (and her feelings) and stopped speaking. After some investigation, we found that Maxime's mother had done exactly the same thing herself, as had her grandmother, and her grandmother's mother, back through time. Lining up 'the women', Maxime found light out beyond the 'ancestral line' and one by one brought the light through to radiate and dissolve the forms. Bringing all this light into the mother form, she was transformed and Maxime cried her mother's tears plus her own tears of relief. Little Maxime was then reconciled with her mother, and Maxime found her energy. As she began to radiate, she became a

beacon of light and all the energy expanded in adult Maxime's throat. She coughed and felt her throat 'inflamed' momentarily until it cooled to 'beautiful stillness'. Within weeks, the pre-cancerous condition disappeared. More surprising to her was that her estranged mother, living in another country, called after the session and announced that she had put herself into therapy, something her version of her faith had never permitted. Healing an 'inner other' often seems to affect the 'other' in the outer world (see Absent Healing, Chapter Fourteen).

Annie's story

Anorexia *'I feel starved of love, yet everyone around me is very concerned for me.'*
Annie was painfully thin and had been diagnosed anorexic. She had tried many ways of resolving her eating disorder, all unsuccessful.

After some searching we found Annie's five-year-old self behind her, still in 'Australia'. This was the happy child who had split because she was so upset at being forced to move continents. Feeling something missing and eating to comfort herself, then feeling disgusted with her physical appearance, which she perceived as 'fat', she relieved herself of the food, the 'weight' by not eating. (People in Annie's situation will either diet, often to the point of starvation, or throw up after they have eaten, refusing to take in nourishment, or rejecting whatever they do eat.) Back in 'Australia', back in her past, located several feet behind her body, the five year old 'waited', 'starved of company', suddenly alone, in limbo, existing but not alive. Having her 28-year-old self travel to 'Australia' in her mind's eye, she collected the five year old and brought her to the present. In a second session, having had a week for the five-year-old and the 28-year-old selves to get to know one another, she integrated the missing younger energy fully into her adult self. The anorexia ceased. Annie told her story, including putting photographs of her previously emaciated body, in a newspaper colour supplement to help others understand the disease and be heartened by her return to health. Annie achieved an appropriate body weight and took a job meeting the public.

Barbara's story

Brain tumour *'I am willing to sacrifice myself for my children.'*
Barbara did not come to us because of illness. She was a sales
manager who had worked with us to learn to manage people
effectively. In that session she recovered her 'authority and strength'
from a seven-year-old self lost in her convent school days. Two years
later, she came to see us again when she was pregnant with twins.
The doctors were very worried about one of the babies. Talking
telepathically to the twins, she uncovered a past life story where the
two had drowned in Canada in a fishing accident in the 1800s. The
brother who had tried to save his drowning sibling was the ailing
baby, trying to make up for that life. She healed the men back in that
life by finding their light and having it expand, dissolving the forms and
the energy radiated through the babies and her stomach. Soon after,
she telephoned to say that the ailing twin was recovering and
strengthening.

During the phone call, Barbara mentioned that she had been having
headaches which had developed during the two years since we had
originally seen her and which she had not mentioned when working
on the twins. She scheduled a next appointment which was cancelled
as she was retaining fluid and had been prescribed bed rest.

The twins were born, but within hours Barbara herself died of a brain
tumour. Not all situations have a totally happy ending and we have to
accept this. We do wonder what might have happened if she had
managed to keep the appointment.

Clive's story

Chest pains *'I feel as if my heart is hurting.'*
We have included one of Clive's own experiences as it illustrates
how a 'past life' can permeate several realities with ill effects (literally)
in this life. Clive had awoken from a dream, where he was 'murdering'
two children. Dream analysis usually suggests that everything in our
dreams represents a part of us, and that dreams are a way of our
unconscious signalling something that needs to be cleared. This dream
was so vivid, and the physical pain so real, that we did some work

with it right there in bed. (Clive had previously been for tests and his heart and lungs were perfectly normal.)

We used his chest as the doorway it had clearly signalled itself to be and with inner eyes looked in. Beyond his back (he could feel a sensation between his shoulder blades), he saw poster paint quality colours, first black, then red, then green, then yellow, each a layer of protection, one behind the other. As each colour gave way to the next, he felt the pain in his body go lower until it reached his stomach. Yellow opened to the scene of the father and two children in plague-ridden Europe in the Middle Ages. The demented father, dying with plague, and following his wife's death, was putting the children beyond misery and burying their bodies. Finding white light in the man and the children, which became one, this energy spoke of its experience of being in body and how for eleven lifetimes after this one, it had stayed hidden causing various physical and emotional problems. It showed Clive the intervening lives, many ordinary, some highborn. When the light came through into Clive he spoke of his chest expanding. Whatever one believes about past lives, the symptoms disappeared. To the client, the experiences are real, and they certainly have real benefits.

Lara's story*

Chronic digestive problems and acidosis *'I took charge of my life and stepped on any sensitive feelings.'*

From childhood (age 5 to 6), Lara experienced severe constipation and stomach cramps. By late teens this became nervous anxiety, acid stomach, difficulty in keeping food down and 'indigestion from hell.' A stomach ulcer was suspected and antibiotics prescribed, which eased the symptoms, but when they stopped, the symptoms returned. At age 25, Lara saw a homeopath. The first interview was a disaster, but Lara did listen to the advice to stop eating meat. Symptoms lessened and she realised that the homeopath had helped her to uncover some 'emotional baggage'.

At age 28, Lara sought help from an associate who used the

*Lara's story was first published in *Positive Health* in June 1999.

Ravenscroft Approach (as RAPSI was then called) with her over five sessions in 1995. Lara resolved a number of family issues, finding an inner small child and father, which dissolved back into her energy and provided her with some peace of mind. However, the stomach problems continued, and in January 1996, a complementary health specialist in London applied something called the 'HLB test' and provided the first blood scan, which showed the acidic and stressed condition of her stomach.

Lara decided not to take the medicine prescribed but to undertake further work at our centre, which is when the two of us first became involved. She clearly believed that the symptoms and the root cause could be discovered and resolved. Not knowing about the medical tests, we saw her for six sessions in March and April 1996, ending on the 25th April. On the 19th April, Lara had her second test with the health specialist, which showed that her condition had reached a climax, its worst point (in our terms a healing crisis). The third test on the 10th June showed that the condition had completely cleared. This was still the case in 2002 when we re-established contact with Lara and found her happily married, with a child and running a thriving coaching and consultancy business. At the end of her sessions with us, Lara shared the medical evidence with us (see diagrams on the colour pages).

The first four sessions with us involved a great deal of further healing and releasing of the protected and protecting energies that populated her system.

The fifth session on 16th April brought her face to face with a 'controller' in the back of her head (she kept touching the back of her head unconsciously, she had noticed heaviness and tightness in that area, and we also felt it in our bodies as we energetically matched her system), whose mission was 'to struggle'. For a week, in between sessions, she lived with the realisation of how she was leading her life (at this point, her blood test showed the worst stage of her condition). By the sixth and final session, Lara fully understood that the deepest cause of her physical symptoms was a pattern of struggle. The Unconscious Equation (see Chapter Eight) in this case was that struggle = achievement.

Behind her body-self, the her sitting on the chair, Lara found another self, aged 14, still acting out the beliefs that she had learned from her family. Looking into the form of the 14 year old with x-ray vision, she saw 'light below her feet', hidden there when 'she took charge of her life and stepped on any sensitive feelings'.

After acknowledgement and dialogue, the light was freed to flow into the 14-year-old form, creating a radiating being, which dissolved into pure energy which flowed into the back of Lara's throat and then up and down her physical body. *'I feel I can breathe at last,'* she said. The physical change in her outward appearance was also obvious – her skin tone and facial expression changed and there was a general softening of the body posture. *'My acidosis will clear in six weeks,'* she predicted*. Six weeks later on the 10th June, Lara had her last HLB test, and the acidosis had gone.

Some time later, Lara talked about the total experience and she summed it up by saying, *'I want people to know what is possible. Given my symptoms and experience it would have been easy to give up and think that I could not change, that things could not be different, and given my struggle pattern, that was true. However, I found the root cause and the symptoms have vanished. It's so nice not to be ill any more, it's also so nice to feel how I feel inside and to view life as I now view it. Something has manifested on the physical level. A lot more things have manifested on an emotional, mental and psychological level.'*

The reason that Lara could not 'dump her emotional baggage' and that it continued to communicate with her through her symptoms, was that there was a part of her that would not be dismissed like some unwanted 'baggage', and was, in fact, the source of her release and healing. It was the missing potential that she, as a senior executive, had been both searching for and compensating for through obsessive and stress-producing work. Like the relief that you feel when lost luggage is found by the airline, when you are travelling, in this case, on the road of life, Lara was finally able to begin her 'holiday' and that relaxation now permeates her being, her behaviours and her life, till this day.

---

* We frequently ask people to predict when a condition will clear up, or how many sessions they will need with us and they are almost always accurate. Intuition can be trusted.

Chapter Sixteen

Obsessions and addictions

There are many unwanted and self-abusive behaviours that can be looked at on a spectrum from severe to mild, from literally tearing one's hair out or washing in Dettol, to biting one's nails and obsessively making lists. They have two things in common, something is trying to get one's attention and something is doing the best it can to maintain control in a world which was and still is perceived to be a threat.

Obsessive and compulsive behaviour takes many forms, from avoiding walking on the cracks in the pavement, to being obsessed with another person. What we know is that however much the person in adult life tries to stop the behaviour, something behind the scenes maintains it and it is motivated by an underlying positive intention and need. Something the person desperately wants and needs is control, familiarity, the feeling of safety.

Most treatments deal with the symptoms, trying to get the person to modify or control the behaviours, and we have talked to one support group for sufferers who were clinging to each other and to the familiarity of the group. There was a strong message: *'Please don't distract me. I have my coping mechanisms and I am terrified that if I mess with them my symptoms will increase.'*

Addictions are much the same in origin and again we are talking about a specific behaviour such as drinking excessively, smoking, indiscriminate sex, obsessive shopping, gambling, continuously playing computer games, etc. They all attempt to fill a need, and universally do not fully satisfy that need and can be harmful to one's health, bank balance or social standing.

Habits seem mild by comparison, from nail biting and general untidiness to incompletions such as leaving the top off the toothpaste tube.

So how do the symptoms show up and what was it that each person discovered when they started exploring?

Steve's story

'I am tearing my hair out.'

This was literally the case and in Steve's outer world he was having problems with the roof of his house! It was not rocket science to wonder if there was something 'up and out' trying to get his attention, and in the first few moments of the session, unconsciously he placed his hand on the top of his head several times to illustrate points he was making. On investigation, the basic construct (energetic structure) involved the energy of him as a small child who had escaped the body (*'I feel sometimes that I am crawling out of my body'*; he already had!) and a hysterical mother (created out of his energy at that young age) who was 'hitting the roof' and 'tearing her hair out' at something minor he did (washing his hair with the wrong shampoo).

It was so easy to see where the problem had originated and where to start work. However, there was something else as yet unknown in control of the compulsive behaviour and this part was fiercely holding on to this behaviour. The compulsive behaviour had to remain as a sign that this place existed. To compensate, the person was then dealing with the symptoms of the behaviour rather than the cause (the energetic fragment).

There was a positive benefit. His Unconscious Equation (see Chapter Eight) was that he holds on to controlling himself (not tearing his hair out) so that he is well enough to talk about his problem, get noticed and be loved. He had to keep the symptom, so that it could be controlled, which in his unconscious equalled being loved.

Was this strategy working? Well, partially, yes. He had a support system of loving friends who rallied round, and he got a degree of celebrity status by being interviewed on radio about his 'interesting condition' and how he controlled the behaviour, but he felt he looked a mess and could not attract a partner. Willing now to look up above his head, he found the child and through two sessions began to work to heal the mother so that the light above could merge with the light inside. However, as the healing began, another layer made itself known and his urge to pull hair increased. He withdrew from sessions to 'normalise' his situation, take herbal remedies, get psychic help and maintain the status quo. This work is not a one-stop miracle cure and in severe cases, a healing crisis may be needed, but it can only be completed if the client continues with sessions. Was this a failure? In terms of fully clearing the behaviour, yes. In terms of the larger picture, no. Shortly afterwards, his hair started to grow back, he met someone and was beginning a relationship. His controller is still making itself evident but there had clearly been some movement.

Carol's story

'I drink to blot out my life.'

Drinking was Carol's presenting problem and we immediately wanted to know the bottom line. What is important about blotting out your life? The answer was, *'so that I feel OK about myself'*. There was a clear I and Self/Myself split.

She came for 10 sessions. By the 10th session she had located and integrated 80% of herself, and then she owned up to a deeper addiction, sex. The language was graphic and her need for male penetration was clear. Having her 'look up' her own vagina, (in her mind's eye) she found a dark red energy and she said, 'It comes and it goes' (which also described the behaviour of her male consorts). Looking into the energy, she found her 16-year-old self who had been jilted at the altar. It was her feelings of the loss of and the need for love which was, at least partially, driving her obsession.

In that area she discovered the forms of the man who jilted her and all the subsequent men who had taken advantage of her or whom she had used for temporary relief. Healing and releasing her masculine and her feminine energy produced a wave of relief, which she knew was the orgasmic feeling that she had been searching for.

David's story

'I am reluctant to commit myself.'

30 per cent of David was positively committed while 70 per cent was committed to being cut off, to escape and to protection. He felt easily distracted and not good enough. He smoked and overate. His 70 per cent was being critical and analytical. It also made him untidy – and it had a sense of humour.

His mother and father had split up and his aunt, who had been a chambermaid in a big house, brought him up. He marked out his heart and his stomach with gestures as he spoke. He found a lot of energy below his feet, uncommitted to him and his life. The dark light down there felt depressed, bleak, lonely, weighty. (Notice the language - something waiting usually links to the person's weight as they weigh themselves down, until they find the energy down below which comes up to lighten them.) The dark layer was protecting the light by stopping it coming up. The positive intention was to stop him achieving which in his mind would keep him from possible failure, so as to keep him safe (the Unconscious Equation). In three sessions he found this light, and the light through his chest which was holding him back, and the energy in his stomach into which the act of smoking helped him breathe. Smoking as a way of bringing breath to an area (chest, stomach) where a part of the person's energy is trapped, is very common. Ask when the energy became trapped there, and you get the age at which an insecure teenager started to smoke, not realising that inside him or herself was a younger self feeling unworthy.

David started to smoke when he was 20, and sure enough, inside his stomach was a 20-year-old self, feeling anxious and tense. Inside the 20 year old was an eighteen-month-old toddler. The toddler's light was released, radiating through the 20 year old and filling the adult. 'I feel that my compulsion had melted away', he said, which is paradoxical because in 'becoming' part of the present, there is a 'going', 'leaving', 'melting away' of a symptom. It is precisely because people try to deny or 'get rid' of a symptom that it may strengthen, or reappear as something else, and the process actually needs a 'finding of the light and a becoming' to enable that 'going' to happen. Does applying a palliative patch to remove the chemical drive to smoke actually remove the origin of the continuing behaviour? We suspect not.

Simon's story

'I don't belong here. I feel that I was not totally born.'

Having experienced a personal tragedy at the age of five, it took 25 years for the adult to realise that he had managed to survive with only part of himself available. His obsessive compulsive behaviour was that he would become fixated on an object and stare at it, drawing on its life force until he was finally able to tear himself away.

In his first sessions he found and talked to the energy which he found back right, outside his body, which felt oppressive and controlling and pushing him. He also spoke to the five year old who was out front left in his own little world, which Simon experienced as a 'bubble'. He integrated the light from the two images and for one day felt whole, which encouraged him to continue living. Previously he had considered suicide an option. He was also able to decide to move from the business world to become a therapist. He knows that his own further healing and coming to wholeness will form part of his learning process.

Jackie and Cindy's stories

I feel dirty.

Two different clients made the same statement. One, Jackie, who made a mistake as a teenager, was sexually molested. The other, Cindy, got lice while at school.

Jackie's behaviour was obsessive cleaning of her body, even using antiseptic until her skin bled. Cindy cleaned her house obsessively and washed her hair sometimes two and three times a day. In both cases the adult was trying to maintain a normal face to the world, while the inner teenager felt dirty because of what had happened in the past. In one case we got through to the teenager and she unlocked the energetic door, which she had locked from the inside. The other case had not been resolved at the time of writing as she was still stuck in a Negative Dependency (see Chapter Nine). It's not always easy to wean oneself off a habit which seems to bring some benefits.

Fiona's story

I am bloated and have wind and my stomach gets into knots.

Literal listening was our way in to this problem. Inside Fiona was the anorexic teenage her, '(k)not' eating, '(k)not' being fully in the world, and making knots in the adult's energy system! A lot of (k)nots. She recovered and healed the teenager, releasing the light, which expanded through her belly, which could then contract and no longer be bloated.

Dale's story

'I used to challenge myself to complete everything on my to-do list, however long it took and however tired I was.'

Although this trait was seen as admirable at Dale's place of work, it indicated a conflict between 'I', who did the challenging, and 'myself', who was running along trying to keep up and was permanently tired. There was also a third part monitoring the behaviour. When all three were reconciled with one another and radiating, they brought unity and a sense of true balance, as opposed to the seesaw effect of doing and stopping that Dale experienced. This also paved the way to helping Dale see a new way of working. He became more calm, planned better, learnt to say no to unrealistic deadlines and completed priority jobs first.

Pat's story

'I cannot stop biting my nails.'

A past life where the person starved to death was the root cause of this 'gnawing' and annoying behaviour. When we released the light and brought it through so that it was radiating through Pat, she gradually stopped biting her nails.

Chapter Seventeen

If it ain't broke ...

There are generally two kinds of people: those who see the glass of life half full, and those for whom it seems half empty. Those who feel 'half empty' or 'less-than' are usually forced by circumstances – material or health – to recognise that they have problems and they may well seek help. For others material circumstance may lull them into a false sense of security for a while, or even a good part of their lives. They as a result do not feel they need to put much effort into their inner lives.

They generally perceive their lives to be working well. They have material success and positions of influence, and few, if any, symptoms of dis-ease: perhaps some stress in the family, some aches and pains. They may, however, compartmentalise their lives, reserving their caring, nurturing sides for when they are at home, while being known as striving, driving and ruthless in their professional lives. They may be frequently forward looking and goal orientated – and very, very busy. And it isn't done to admit to 'weakness'. When we offered some stress release programmes to a large company some years back, only women came to the free sessions, and then only those at a relatively junior level. It was a weakness to admit to being stressed, and the last thing anyone would think of doing publicly, or at all, was to go for 'therapy'. However what is driving them is frequently a feeling that there has to be something more, something that will make them feel complete, fully satisfied, fulfilled. It generally takes a major problem – too much stress, a breakdown, divorce, a 'mid-life crisis' – to bring such people to therapy. But it needn't be this way. We are all fragmented. Our goal is that people find, release and fully embody their trapped energy before it makes itself known as a problem. So even if it ain't broke yet, fix it!

So what is the attraction of this work in professional circles? Since the 60s there has been a growth in management science and the understanding of emotional intelligence. Interest in personal development has increased dramatically, and although therapy is still not acceptable for many, there is a current vogue for hiring a life coach. People know that they could be more. They strive for excellence.

For many, though, excellence means 'performance excellence', which in turn means 'success in the material world'. But many people who seem to be performing well on the outside are actually in conflict on the inside of feeling inadequate, fraudulent and dissatisfied. This can lead to workaholism, over-reacting, declining relationships and ill-health. If the feelings on the inside are played out on the outside, we have the company chairman who pretends to be an adult but has tantrums like a four year old. Their behaviour is being influenced by a fragmented and unhappy inner world. From the struggle, stress and distress of being fragmented, we get men and women behaving badly. Is it any wonder that leadership in so many fields of endeavour has a bad name because the person or the group in charge abuses the power which comes with the position. However good our intentions, however much we try to train our minds to focus on positive behaviour, if we do not release our untapped energies and frustrated potential, at best we hold ourselves back and at worst we hurt ourselves and others. You've heard the expression 'feel the fear and do it anyway'. We say 'feel the fear, release its cause and do it easily'.

What is common to all the examples which follow, and many others we could mention, is that each person was successful in professional and material terms. Each wanted to develop themselves and even if there had had been a sharp wake-up call in some cases, none of them would have 'normally' been considered a case for 'therapy', yet they chose to do some evolving and we congratulate them.

Ben's story

Ben, a multi-millionaire businessman and world-class sportsman, who was renowned for the ruthless way he conducted business, shocked himself by losing $2m on a deal. He discovered in a session with Clive that he had shut down his 'compassion'. This comprised 50% of himself which was mostly located in his right hemisphere/brain and in his heart. He also had a mild heart murmur!

With RAPSI, he recovered and released his compassionate heart energy and resolved to combine his business acumen with his new understanding of 'the human condition'. He went on to found a successful health products business.

Jacqui's story

The CEO-designate of the UK subsidiary of a global food manufacturing business, Jacqui was 'cool' when dealing with potential board colleagues. We found her 'Victorian' ancestors installed in the back of her head. They were her her unconscious benchmark for professional behaviour and she was using them to judge herself and spur herself on. The RAPSI work involved freeing the energy that it took to keep this structure in place, which manifested as an energetic rod up her spine and into her brainstem, like a secondary backbone. In its place, she found her 'warmth' which allowed her to unwind and soften. Thereafter she developed a more charismatic and more effective style of leadership.

Henry's story

Henry was the bids Director for an international IT business. He was in charge of teams which secured contracts in the hundreds of millions of pounds and was being groomed to be an Industry Director with main board responsibility. He wasn't happy about his 'killer instinct' and after some RAPSI sessions he put in place a more collaborative style of leadership. If he had not found, standing behind him, the origins of his success as a teenager fighting for his ethnic rights on the streets of London, he would be fighting boardroom battles still. Shortly after our sessions, he was headhunted to lead a new IT business.

Iain's story

Iain was a Director in a company Clive was working with who happened to ask Clive about his coaching work. As an illustration, Clive asked Ian look into the area of his stomach, since he had said previously that he had an ulcer. To his surprise, Iain found two family members there. Some hours later he called Clive at home, in amazement, joy and relief that over dinner his 'inner family members' had telepathically communicated his 'worth' to him. He heard thewords and felt an upsurge of wonderful energy. He said he was suddenly feeling much less anxious and was looking forward to much easier interactions with others.

Mary's story

Mary was a budding director who wanted to develop her people management skills. She had a razor sharp attention to detail, but lacked coaching skills and a light touch. To her surprise she found that her ability to bond with people and create rapport were resident in a happy eight-year-old self who was still standing on the shores of Ireland, as another eight-year-old, weeping for the loss of home, sailed away to grow to adulthood in England. She integrated the energy of the inner child and became a charismatic leader. Shortly afterwards she was appointed Managing Director.

Some time later, she started a family and at seven months pregnant she had her last coaching session before taking maternity leave. She said she was very tired and that the baby was lying awkwardly, which was evident from her ungainly walk and lopsided stomach. She was asked to look into her stomach, see the baby and talk to it. She learned that the baby was uncomfortable, pushed to the side, and that there was a grey cloud in the space where it was supposed to be. Passionate about having her first child, she was concerned to learn that the grey cloud represented ambivalence about being a mother. However, it was her mother's ambivalence about having her that she was feeling, a sensation she had felt as a foetus in her mother's womb and retained through to adulthood. She found the light in the child and in the grey cloud, and saw their energy expand through her stomach and womb. We both saw, and she felt, the baby shift visibly. From then on, instead of having to go home early each evening to rest, she had bags of energy. She resumed being the cox for a rowing team, and carried on till near the delivery, which was quick and trouble free. We can attest to the vitality and calmness of the baby and to the easy birth of her next child.

Bonnie's story

A young, seemingly successful businesswoman with everything to live for, Bonnie had nevertheless attempted suicide. *'I can see no point in living,'* she said when she came to us.

So who was speaking and from where? Over and over again we ask this question. In many cases the answer will be from a part of the self from this lifetime. In other cases, it may be a person looking beyond a 'doorway', signalled by a tightness in the chest, a feeling in the head, etc, into another time. It transpired that in Bonnie's case it was a little girl in Victorian England whose teacher had brutalised her and caused her death. The teacher had killed himself. The guilt-ridden father who had employed the teacher, the teacher and the child all needed healing. This involved finding and bringing out the light, but only after a lot of interaction and discussion, expressed anger and then forgiveness between the three. Did we induce a trance and take her on a specific journey? Not formally, but clients frequently transport themselves to an altered state induced by our questions. Bonnie spontaneously found in her and around her everything she needed to be healed. Bonnie realised that the words she heard 'there is no point in living' were the words of the child. In some circles this might be called a spirit attachment. We see it as part of the larger self and by healing the forms and releasing the energy, it can be recycled into the present bringing Bonnie, in this case, all the deep feelings of relief, peace and understanding. Subsequently she herself became a teacher.

Simon's story

'What am I supposed to do with this little green man in the back of my head?' Not everyone is prepared for what they find! This market research manager went on to find his young four-year-old self who had created the image of the green man which he had seen on television in the 70s. The four year old held his creative spark. To say he was pleased wit hthe discovery and unleashing of his creativity is a gross understatement.

Alexander's story

The chairman of a consulting firm discovered that the fragmentation and conflict within his business, and also his marriage, directly correlated to the fragmentation and conflicts within himself. 'I have experienced falling apart and putting myself back together again,' he said. He then reconstructed his business, and his marriage improved.

Jake's story

A local authority professional who was very good at his job, Jake wanted to feel more involved and engaged with colleagues in social situations. The root cause went back to the time when, aged five, he left Africa where he had been treated as a precious child, only to arrive in this country to be bullied and abused, a pattern which was repeated as he tried to fit in with English society. Part of him had stayed behind in Africa and part of him was still reliving a nasty hospital experience he'd had as a child in the UK. After the first session his whole face looked different. Where he had looked rather drawn, and one side of his mouth drooped to give him a noticeably despondent look, his face seemed to fill out and his mouth evened up so that he smiled easily.

When the people in this chapter came to work with us, they had all achieved a degree of success in their lives. They did not consider themselves 'broken', nor were they. Yet they discovered a fragmented structure, their internal universe, and they began to find fragments of themselves that they didn't know were there and which they hadn't consciously missed. So why start probing if it isn't hurting? Because you can fix it before it becomes a problem, and because at some level 'it' is hurting. Maintaining a fragmented structure results in compensatory behaviours with negative results and takes energy – from yourself and from others. So if you think you feel good now, why not feel even better?

Those around you will benefit too. Those people who have chosen roles in society where they are responsible for or to others (politicians, world leaders, opinion formers, teachers, doctors, etc) owe it to others to start their inner journey.

Each journey follows a similar pattern, although the content and sequence of anyone's journey will be unique. That is why the Wholeness Programme which follows should be treated as a series of signposts. The order in which your journey progresses will depend on many different circumstances relating only to you, just as each journey with a client follows where they lead.

The thing that every journey has in common though is the destination – wholeness.

Chapter Eighteen

The final piece

Throughout this book we have been saying that the way the light hides itself is its way of protecting itself. That was the story that seemed to emerge from clients' journeys, and that does still seem to be true. However we have now discovered that that is not the whole story.

Whenever a client reaches the source of pure light which is the essence of them and which essentially is them, we facilitate them to have a conversation with it before helping it release and bringing it through to embodiment. What we came to realise was that in different ways the source light kept saying that it always hides itself behind these layers of protection (they are indeed protection), that this is a fundamental part of the human story. For one example, look at Anna's story on page 88. Eileen asked the light, Who created the dimensions?

L *I did.*

E *Why?*

L *It happens as part of the process of creating the human form.*

The light says something similar every time we ask.

This journey of inner discovery is one we are all meant to make. It is the route to spiritual realisation. It is the light's way of experiencing itself, of fully realising itself, of becoming manifest. As the physical and metaphysical aspects of the human being combine, we become who we were truly meant to be. The fragmented energetic structure is one of the basic building blocks of a human being. It is our job to find, reintegrate, embody and radiate the light so that we and the light can experience what it means to be fully human.

The inner journey is no longer something for the few people who decide to take it.

It is the life purpose of every one of us.

Wholeness Programme

The Wholeness Programme offers you a series of exercises to allow you to practise some of the RAPSI process. In order to get the most benefit, it is important to have read the book first so that you have a clear idea of what RAPSI entails, and then that you do all the exercises, without skipping any, in the order given.

Buy a new notebook to use as your RAPSI journal, or make sure that you keep everything you write, as your work in the early exercises forms the basis of some of the later exercises. Take as long as you need to work through the programme, making sure you take at least two weeks to give your system time to adjust to any changes.

We also recommend that you write down your recollection of any inner journeying you do. If at any stage you get stuck, thank yourself and your system for the work you have done and write an account of it. At a later time, come back to it and compare your session with some of the case studies in the book. This might give you some pointers as to the sorts of questions and techniques you might use to continue the work. Although it is more satisfying to reach a natural conclusion to internal journeying before you stop, there is no reason why you cannot go back to a session, apologise to the parts and say when you will continue if you have to stop in the middle for some reason.

We are well aware that it is a very different matter to explore your own inner universe working alone from a book rather than being guided by a skilled facilitator. We cannot guarantee that you will reach wholeness this way, but from our experience with trainee facilitators we are confident that you will be able to do a lot of productive work.

The difficulty of working alone is that the energy we want to find, release and re-absorb is hidden. And it's hidden as well from you and your system as from the rest of the world. If it was easy to find, we assume many of you would already have done so. We are asking the very system that has done the hiding to explore itself. This is particularly true when it comes to integrating the observers – those parts that may even think they are the only 'you'.

We (Eileen and Clive) facilitate each other, so if you have a friend or friends you could do this work with, you may find that two or more people are better at asking probing questions than one. If you're alone, then you might experiment early on with the 'chair' technique explained in Exercise 20.

Whatever you are able to do is a step in the right direction. And please do feel free to contact us through our website (www.rapsi.org) if you need help or would like to tell us about your experiences.

Enjoy the journey! We look forward to hearing from you.

Exercise 1 Why am I doing this?

5 minutes

Before starting this exercise, read the relevant section on page 28.

Sit quietly, take a deep breath, close your eyes and relax. Ask yourself why you are choosing to do this programme of exploration. What has prompted you to improve your life? In your journal, write down whatever words come to you. Write as much as you can in the time.

Read what you have written. Acknowledge it. Take responsibility – and then get curious.

Thank yourself for starting this programme of self discovery.

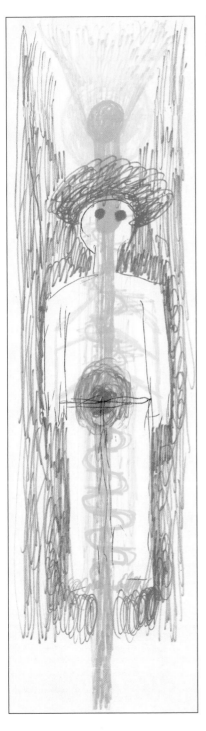

Energy maps produced by RAPSI workshop participants as a result of 'body scanning' (see page 40 and Exercise 13 on page 158).

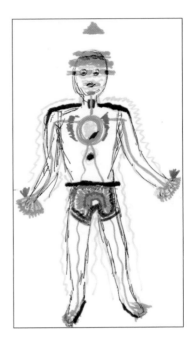

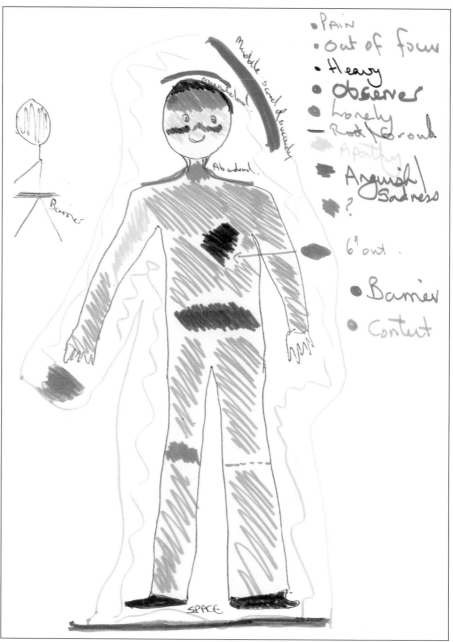

An energy map produced by a RAPSI workshop participant as a result of body scanning, where she looked with inner eyes to discover pockets and stashes of trapped energy in her system. She was able to name the different types of energy trapped in and around her body (see page 40 and Exercise 13 on page 158).

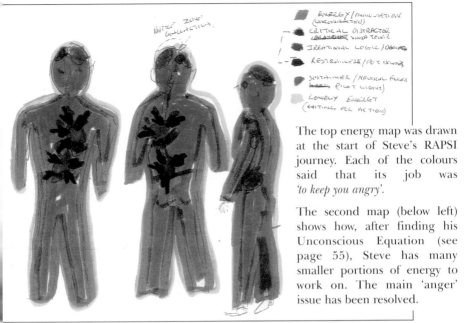

The top energy map was drawn at the start of Steve's RAPSI journey. Each of the colours said that its job was *'to keep you angry'*.

The second map (below left) shows how, after finding his Unconscious Equation (see page 55), Steve has many smaller portions of energy to work on. The main 'anger' issue has been resolved.

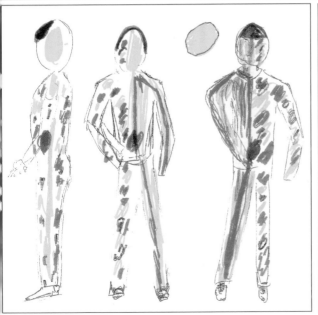

The third map (right) after more RAPSI work shows much more cohesion and balance in Steve's energetic system as many of his issues are resolved. Steve's fourth map was a body in outline only – no colours, only white. Steve felt that he was at 10, radiating.

1st test – 28th January 1996

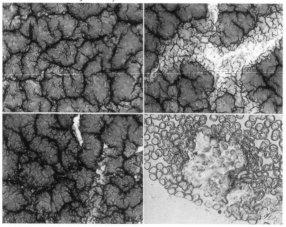

These are the results of Lara's blood work (see Lara's story, page 125) showing her stomach problems and the progress of her healing during her RAPSI therapy. The top pictures indicate her illness when she started working with us.

The middle pictures were produced at a mid-point during her therapy when we felt she was experiencing a healing crisis.

The final set of pictures, showing healthy blood, was produced six weeks after we finished working with her, the time she had predicted for being healed.

Lara had decided to take no medication, and trust only in her internal exploration and release work. We did not know about the blood tests until after our final session with her.

2nd test – 19th April 1996

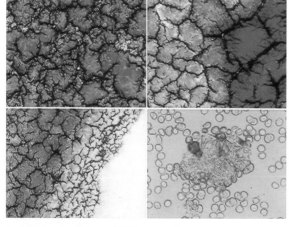

Key to the four pictures

Stress	Lymph
Stomach	Free Radicals

3rd test – 10th June 1996

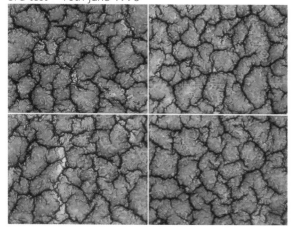

HLB is a morphological blood-sedimentation test which enables a diagnosis from 2 to 3 drops of blood using phase-contrast microscopy, oberving patterns of blood coagulation profiles. Healthy cells look a red uniform red colour. Pathology is indicated by white gaps between the red cells.

Exercise 2 How well is my life working now?

5 minutes

Before starting this exercise, read the relevant section on page 29.

In your journal, on a scale of 1 to 10 (where 10 is fully satisfied), rate how satisfied you are on average with the following areas of your life. If you're not sure, go with your gut feeling or your first response.

Add headings to fit yourself and your own life, eg religion, work colleagues, individual children, and friends by name, etc.

- Self
- Partner
- Children
- Family
- Friends/others
- Health
- Work
- Finances
- Living environment
- Leisure Time
- Clarity of purpose
- Sense of well-being

Write down any comments you have about these scores.

Thank yourself for taking the time to do this exercise.

Exercise 3 Problems, challenges and issues

10-15 minutes

Before starting this exercise, read the relevant section on page 30.

Write down any problems, challenges or issues in your life at the moment as you perceive them. Give your first instinctive answers. State these in as many ways as are relevant and appropriate. Be as specific as possible as well as giving the general picture and sense. The more you write, the more clues you will have later to help you find your 'missing piece/s'.

Thank yourself for doing the exercise. Tell yourself when you will continue with the next exercise.

Exercise 4 Evidence

15-20 minutes

Deepen your awareness further. What is your evidence for what you have written so far? Think of incidents in the present or the past. How do you feel? What has happened to you? What would others (especially significant others) say about you and your problems?

Again, write as much as you can, using the first words that come into your mind.

Here are some questions to get you started:
- *Where have I compromised myself in my life?*
- *What secrets do I keep? Which bits do I keep hidden?*
- *If my life ended right now, what regrets would I have?*
- *What do I complain about?*
- *Who do I blame and for what?*
- *What habits do I have that I would like to change?*
- *What obsessions do I have? Food, alcohol, drugs, shopping, sex, work, caring for others ...?*
- *Am I accident prone? In what way?*
- *Am I a victim? In what way?*
- *How is my health? When in my life has it not been good?*
- *Who do I most take after – parents, grandparents, who? What do I like, dislike about the similarities?*
- *What would make life better?*
- *What would make life perfect?*
- *Is it possible to be perfect? What is perfection? How could I achieve it? How do I know this?*
- *On a scale of 1 to 10 (10 is fully in the present), how much of me on average is fully present, grounded in the moment?*
- *Any other question/s you want to add ...?*

Thank yourself for taking the time to do this exercise. Tell yourself when you will continue with the next exercise.

Exercise 5 Recurring Negative Feelings

5 minutes

Before starting this exercise, read the relevant section on page 30.

What negative feelings (fear, loneliness, shame, etc) are chronically with you as an undercurrent, running in the background? What negative feelings have shown up when you least expected them?

We call these your CNDs, 'chronic negative deposits. You will use them later in an exercise to find your Unconscious Equation.

For now, list them, all of them.

Feel free to take a break between exercises. Thank yourself for the work you have done so far.

Exercise 6 Your relationship with yourself

10 minutes

Before starting this exercise, read the relevant section on page 31.

As always, find some quiet space and time. Take a deep breath and relax quietly and ask yourself the following questions:

How do I feel about myself?

What do I think about myself?

What would my parent(s) say about me?

And my partner, my children, any other significant person/s in my life?

Write as much as you can in the time.

Thank your system for helping you explore these questions.

Exercise 7 I/Self statements

10 minutes

Before starting this exercise, read the relevant section on page 31.

In as many ways as possible in the time available, complete the sentence
'I .... myself'.
eg I love myself.
   I don't understand myself.

It does not matter if some of your statements seem to contradict one another.
Write everything that comes to mind which seems in any way to be true.

Thank yourself for taking the time to do this exercise. Tell yourself when you will continue with the next exercise.

Exercise 8 Desired Outcome

10-20 minutes

Before starting this exercise, read Chapter Five starting on page 33.

Read through all the notes you have made about your questions and answers so far. With all the understanding you have of yourself, it is now time to discover your 'Desired Outcome', what you truly want for yourself.

You can do this activity for your life's purpose or for an interim desire. As you continue to work through the exercises and release more energy to be available to you, revisit your Desired Outcome to see how close you are getting and to see whether you want to revise it.

Start by writing down how you would like your life to be different. Look back at those things you are dissatisfied with and write what you would like to take their place. Be as precise as possible. These questions might help you.

- *Overall on a scale of 1 to 10, how satisfied are you with your life to date? What would make it a 10?*
- *Look forward into the future and see yourself living in a state of '10'. What will it be like? Where will you be living? Who with? Who will your friends be? What will you be doing day to day? What is your Big Dream? What do you want for yourself? What will it look like, sound like, feel like?*
- *What do you sense is your major purpose in this lifetime? Any minor purposes? How are you doing in achieving that purpose?*
- *What sort of person are you deep down? What sort of person do you want to be? How will others describe you? What will they notice about you?*
- *If 'Authentic Excellence' (our definition of '10') is a state of being, of radiating, free of blocks, inner conflicts, withholdings, inauthentic behaviour and dis-ease, how near are you to that state? What would bring you closer to being Authentically Excellent?*

Check that you are describing a sustainable future life – not a situation which would be good for a short holiday from 'real life'. What we're looking for is a state of perfection in your real life.

Thank yourself for taking the time to do this exercise.

Exercise 9 The bottom line

10-20 minutes

Before starting this exercise, read the relevant section on page 34.

Read what you have written as your Desired Outcome in Exercise 8. Ask yourself, *'If I had all of that, what would that give me?'*

And when you have an answer to that question, ask yourself about this new answer: *'And what would that give me?'*

Specifically ask yourself, *'How will I feel if I have all of this?*

Keep questioning your answers until you get to what feels like your 'bottom line' answer – which will probably be expressed as how you want to feel.

Finally ask yourself, *'Is there anything I want to add?'*

Make sure you have written down a clear bottom line Desired Outcome which describes a way of being and feeling, as this is what will fuel what you do, achieve and have. This is what your RAPSI work is leading you towards.

Thank yourself for doing the exercise. Tell yourself when you will continue with the next exercise.

Exercise 10 Questioning your Desired Outcome

5-15 minutes

Before starting this exercise, read the relevant section on page 34.

Take your bottom line Desired Outcome from Exercise 9. Sit quietly and build a rich mental picture or vision of your 'Ideal Future' and the 'Ideal Future You' (the you who is at 10). This will be someone who, for example, is experiencing being 'relaxed, comfortable, peaceful, warm, alive, joyful' (use your own words here). He/she will be energetic and radiating.

How does that Future Self look different from the you of today? Place him/her in different situations in the present, meeting family, going to work, etc, and add some traditionally difficult situations for you from the past. How does he/she handle those situations? What is different?

Ask yourself, *'What can I learn from watching my Future Self?'*

Ask your Future Self some questions and give Future Self permission to answer you telepathically.

• *What advice do you have for me?*
• *What is stopping me from being you right now? How close am I to you in time, age?'*
• *Have I just created you, or have you been there for some time? (How young was I when I created you?)*
• *What is your job?*
• *How do you feel being in my future? How hard do you have to work? Do you get any/enough acknowledgement and thanks?*

Now, keeping Future Self in your mind's eye, check with yourself for any downside of being that Future Self. Ask yourself *'What do I fear I might I lose by becoming my Future Self?'*

Even if your first answer is *'I will lose nothing',* ask some probing questions to help bring up any unconscious fears, eg *'Will I still be recognisable as me? Will my friends and family still like me? Will I want or be able to make new friends? Is this vision just too grand for me? Am I being unrealistic?'*

Now ask, *'What will I gain?'*

What you do next depends on the answers you receive.

If you want to amend your Desired Outcome, go back and, with your new understandings and awareness, repeat Exercises 8, 9 and 10 so you have a bottom line Desired Outcome expressed as positive feelings which your radiant Future Self will already be displaying for you.

If anything in you interfered with you seeing your positive future, thank it and note the fact for use in Exercise 17, The Unconscious Equation.

If you have a bottom line Desired Outcome which has been played out satisfactorily by your Future Self, then proceed to Exercise 11 so you can start the process of integrating the benefits of this positive future.

Thank yourself and your Future Self for doing the exercise. Tell yourself when you will continue with the next exercise.

Exercise 11 Back from the future

Allow 10-20 minutes

Read through the relevant section on pages 36-37, and read through the whole of this exercise before you start.

Be sure you will be undisturbed. Make yourself comfortable, close your eyes and breathe easily and deeply. Get into a calm, quiet state.

Say hello to yourself. Let yourself know that you have positive intentions and want the best for yourself. Your system will get the positive message. At all stages say thank you for any response you get.

Ask whatever part of you that knows how to do this to recreate your Ideal Future Self. See your Future Self facing you. Say 'hello' to your Future Self and get a 'hello' back. Thank your Future Self for being there, for doing its job and for all the help it gave you in the last exercise.

Explain to Future Self that you want it to come into the present, becoming part of you, so that you can begin to create that future. Ask Future Self what it will bring to the relationship. Ask what it will gain from joining with you.

Be respectful of anything it tells you. It is your system and particularly your unconscious aspects which are trying to get through to you, so accept what is said. Your everyday consciousness, sitting back, just needs to remain curious.

Have Future Self help you by looking through you, Present Self, to see if there is any light in and behind you, which will be the same distance behind your body as Future Self is in front of you. This 'bookend' from the past, holding you back or pushing you forward, is the twin to Future Self who pulls you forward. Thank whatever you find and tell it you'd like to bring it into the present. Ask what positive attributes it will bring and what will be resolved.

With your intention invite the Future into now. It could be as simple as Future Self walking into you and expanding through you, bringing the resources to help you create your future.

Alternatively, look into Future Self and see where the light resides. When you can see the light shining, expand it until the form of Future Self dissolves into the light and then draw that light into you. Merge the light of your Future Self with the light at the centre of your Present Self. As you hold that, see the light in Past Self, expand it and draw its light into you to merge with the light of your Present and Future Selves.

Let the light radiate into every fibre of your being and beyond your skin. Enjoy the feeling of strength brought to you by combining with the resources of your Future Self, your past and your present.

Congratulate yourself for bringing this first part of your absent energy into your system.

Exercise 12 Absent healing

Allow 15-30 minutes

Read Chapter Fourteen beginning on page 109 – and read through this whole exercise before you begin.

Take a break from your exploration of yourself to practise some of the basic RAPSI skills through absent healing. (It is often easier to work on other people than on oneself.)

Perhaps, for your first attempt, pick someone who would welcome some emotional support. Thereafter you can do this exercise as often as you like for the same person, or for many different people, living or not living.

Sit and relax. Breathe deeply. Now close your outer eyes (unless you find it easier to concentrate with them open). See the person in your mind's eye, facing you. Say hello to them and ask if they are willing to receive a healing from you. You will typically get agreement. If by some chance you get a no, and if this happens more than once, you may have something in you that is holding beliefs about the process and probably limits you in other ways, so work on yourself first.

You may find that you can simply look in and find the person's light – in which case, go directly to 'Release' on the next page. If not, become curious about where their energy may be hidden, how many protection layers there may be and in what direction/s you may have to look to find it. Allow your intuition and their energy to guide you. Using 'x-ray vision', scan their energetic depths and notice where there is light or dark, where there are concentrations of colour or shapes. You may not see graphic pictures as such, but just get a sense of where to look and work. Maybe a word will pop into your head (stomach, heart), or maybe you know that they have a physical symptom. Look in deeply and acknowledge telepathically or out loud everything that you see – the light and the dark. If you prefer to work graphically, you can draw an energy map (see page 40 and colour pages). Seeing 'nothing' (darkness, void, space, a black hole) in the internal universe is 'something', a part that can be addressed like any other part.

Recognition Say hello to what you see.

Relationship Thank it for being there and for doing its job, which you understand had a positive intention for the person. (You don't need to know what its job is.)

Look through this first layer and notice what you see within or beyond it. Say hello and thank it for being there and for doing its job.

Keep doing this until you find the person's essence – the pure white light. Say hello and thank it for revealing itself. Check that it really is the light at source, or whether there's something more behind it. (Ask it.)

When you are sure that you have reached source, say hello, introduce the light to the person, and vice versa. Introduce the light to the many layers which have been protecting it. Have the light look through the layers to the rest of the light in the person. Have them recognise and say hello to each other.

Reconciliation Ask whether the person, the layers or the lights need to say anything to each other before they merge. If so, allow them to speak and, if necessary, respond until everything that needs to be said has been said.

Release Explain to the light and the person that, in a moment, you will help the hidden light to come forward through the layers and the layers will dissolve back into light. The light will expand, mixing with any light already in the body, and when it reaches the skin line, will continue to expand, radiating out into the world. Ask if everything in the person's system is ready for that to happen.

If you get a no, that will be a part signalling its existence. Get to know it, talk with it, discover its positive intention, etc. Finally it will become part of the healing.

Ask the system if it is ready. If it says no, it will be another part to reconcile, but when the system says it's ready, count to three and then with your intention, draw the light through the layers, dissolving each layer into the light.

Radiating Watch the light expanding, filling the person with light and radiating beyond the person. Notice the effect this has on the person. Ask them telepathically how they feel. Say anything you'd like to say to the person before the vision dissolves. Relax and enjoy the feeling of the healing light.

If you find the healing goes faster than you expect, that's fine. Simply enjoy it. What matters is whether you – and the person you are healing – feel better.

If it's appropriate, check in with the person after this and see how they feel. You can decide whether you want to tell them what you did.

Thank yourself for taking the time and energy to do this exercise and thank the system of the person you have been working with.

Exercise 13 Body scanning and energy mapping

Allow 15-30 minutes

Before starting this exercise, read the relevant sections on page 40 and the colour pages. You need a piece of plain paper (or a clean page in your journal) and some coloured felt-tipped pens or crayons.

The aim is to draw a coloured map representing your energetic structure. You can do this in two ways.

- The first is working in an associated way (you are consciously within your body). Draw three outlines of your body on the page – from the front, from the back and from the side (and a fourth from the other side if there is a significant difference between the two sides). Sense your way through your body from head to toe. Colour in areas of including tension, disease, aches, skin blemishes or any other physical problems in your body. Sense the areas outside your body too which might be considered part of your 'aura'. Trust that your intuition will allow you to do this. Colour in any pieces of energy you sense around you. All of these coloured areas can be considered 'doorways' to hidden energy.

- The second way is working in a dissociated way – sense/seeing yourself from the outside. Use your 'inner eyes'. Start by drawing the three or four outlines of yourself. Then, possibly with some gentle instrumental music playing in the background, settle back in your chair, take a deep breath and relax. Bring to mind an image of yourself of today standing in front of you, facing you. If you have difficulty 'seeing' yourself, try imagining a photo of you, or simply 'sense' yourself.
  Using 'X-ray vision', look into the energy dimensions of the You standing in front of you and visually scan or sense your way through your body. Just notice any impressions you have of colours or shapes. Pay attention to areas of tension or weakness in the body and to things outside the body. Let the colours and shapes come to you.
  Then use the coloured pens and begin to map the areas you have sensed on your outline. Continue until you feel you have finished.
  Follow the same procedure to map your energy from the back and side(s), turning the you out in front of you to give the appropriate view. Note any differences.

Take a moment to consciously thank every colour and shape on your energy maps for its positively-intended job. These are representations of your fragmented energy system and there is a good chance that you have never thanked each one for being part of who you are. Then introduce each colour and shape to the others. Again, these energies will mostly not be aware of the existence of the others. Let them know that they are all part of your energetic system and that they are all doing a positively-intentioned job. Just by doing this, you are already beginning to make connections or reconnections, and you may already feel some positive benefits.

If one of the colours makes itself known through a physical sensation, thank it for its communication and mark it out as one of the first doorways that you will explore.

When you are ready to use the map to find doorways so that you can integrate hidden energy, move on to Exercise 14.

Thank your system for allowing you to do this work, and tell yourself when you will start exploring your energy map.

Exercise 14 Exploring your energy map

Give yourself plenty of time for this exercise; allow up to an hour
Read through the whole exercise before you begin.

You might enjoy doing this exercise with a friend or friends. Other people can often ask more probing questions than you can of yourself, as well as being supportive.

Pick one of the colours in your energy map from Exercise 13. Just choose the piece which most attracts you at the moment. You're going to use this colour as a doorway to journey through to finally discover the white light.

- **Recognition and relationship** Make contact with this colour. Say 'hello'. Thank it for doing its job. Ask what its job is and give it permission to communicate telepathically with you. Ask it if it knows that its most important job is protecting the source of light, yet to be discovered. Thank it for whatever response you get.
- Look through the top layer and see what lies beyond. It may be a colour, an image or yourself as a younger person. Whatever you get, acknowledge it, thank it for doing its job and ask what its job is. You might also ask how long it has been there, whether it is pleased to be found and whether it knew it was going to be found today.

- **Reconciliation** Ask each part if it knows the adult you. If not, tell it today's date and something about your life. Ask it if it knows the previous layer. Introduce the parts to each other, explaining that they are both layers of protection.
  If it seems appropriate, ask each part what it will get from being released into pure light and what it will bring you.
- Look through this layer, and any subsequent layers, repeating the process of acknowledgement, questioning and reconciliation until you discover the white light. Check that it really is the light – ask if there's anything beyond.
- When you're sure you have reached the source light, acknowledge it and thank it for being there. Tell it the date and how old you are. Ask whether it is ready to be released and to bring its energy into the you of today. It is rare for source to decline, but if it does, check whether it is actually source or whether you need to look further. Feel free to ask any other questions you might have.

  Release Have the light look back through the layers to the rest of the light in the you of today and establish communication between the two. Then, with your intention, help to bring the source light through each different layer, dissolving each layer with thanks, until it reaches your body today.
- **Radiating** Have the white light radiate fully all through your body

combining with the light already there, and then continue to radiate the light beyond your skin line so that you are shining out light into the world around you.

- Do a 'feel check'. How do you feel? Is there anything else to do right now before you stop? If so, you can either do it now, following the same process as before, or you can choose to do it later, in which case tell your system when you can resume the process.

Thank yourself and all elements of your system for co-operating in this process of freeing your energies.

After a few days, redraw your body map (do Exercise 13). Notice how it has changed.

You can repeat this exercise as often as you like with different colours in your new body map.

Exercise 15 Literal listening

Allow 10-15 minutes

Before starting this exercise, read the relevant section on page 43.

It can be difficult to listen to yourself as you speak (although the more you try it, the easier it is) so practise by listening to others – listen to people in the street, or on radio or television. However, in this exercise you will be 'literal reading'.

Look back through your journal at all your writings from earlier exercises. Highlight or underline any words or expressions you think might indicate examples of messages from or about your energetic structure, hidden energy, eg *I'm always left behind*, or different parts of you that might need to be integrated, eg *I never stand up for myself.* Who is 'I'? Who is 'myself'?

Write a separate list on a new page of everything you've found. Ignore the context. Resist the temptation to edit. It doesn't matter what you think you meant to say. It's what you did say (or write) that gives the clues to the hidden energy.

Decide whether the words indicate:
- location, eg *something to your left* and *behind you, something up or down* (or both, since something 'up' very often has an opposite piece of energy balancing it at its opposite point 'down'), *something deep in the heart of you,* etc.
- parts of self eg *I don't understand myself sometimes, I was beside myself.*
- watchers, observers or controllers – see Chapter Eleven for examples of the language used by all the different kinds of observers.

When you are ready to use the words to work on integrating hidden energy, move on to Exercise 16 for words relating to location, Exercise 18 for words indicating an I/Self split and Exercise 20 to integrate watchers and observers.

Thank yourself for doing the exercise. Tell yourself when you will continue with your exploration of your inner universe.

Exercise 16 Integrating missing pieces

Allow 30-45 minutes

Use the information from your literal listening in Exercise 15 to locate and integrate missing parts of your energy system.

Follow the 5R sequence in Exercise 14 to locate, integrate and radiate the light.

Your starting point is to choose one of the areas indicated by your listening, eg a piece of energy which is 'up high', and to make it tangible so that you can work with it. You can do this by sitting quietly and sense/seeing what colour it is or what form it takes. Or you can tell yourself that you know there's a doorway there, so sense/see the form the doorway takes. Or you can wonder which voice spoke those words through you and from where, and address it. As soon as you have a tangible form, you can greet it, thank it and form a relationship with it, before looking through it to any further layers of protection.

You can repeat this process as many times as necessary to locate and integrate more missing pieces of your energetic system.

However, as you begin to explore, it is important to remember that this is more than a linear process.

Remember that your energetic system is like a hologram. It is a three-dimensional whole, with pockets of energy within a total energy system. Everything needs to be treated with respect for its positively intended job. Everything needs to get to know everything else. Your job, using your principal consciousness (the you doing the journeying), is to remain curious and to find out the lie of the land, when things happened, what has been the result for you on the outside and for the individual fragments of you in the internal universe, both within your body and outside it. Forming a relationship is not just about being nice, it is about creating the opportunity for things within and outside you to speak, tell you how they feel, express anger if need be, come to peace with another piece of you (child with parents, teacher with student, abused with the abuser, past life with now, something up with something down, back with forward, etc). You need everything to see and speak about things from its perspective.

When you find the light, does it know anything about you? Can it see you, the light in you? What has it been like to be there, possibly for lifetimes, waiting for the rest of itself (of you) to journey to find it. Has it helped you? If so how? (Was it the light that prompted you to buy this book?) What will it bring to you? You get the idea.

Remember too that 'you' are playing the role of detective in your own system and, ultimately, the consciousness which you are using to do the detecting (usually in the head) will need to be fully integrated too – see Exercise 20.

Thank yourself for taking the time to do this exercise and thank your system for co-operating in your exploration of your inner universe.

Exercise 17 Your Unconscious Equation

Allow at least 30 minutes

Read Chapter Eight on the Unconscious Equation (page 55) before you do this exercise.

Your aim is to find out what chronic negative feelings and behaviour you may be holding on to because of their perceived benefits.

• Read again your bottom line Desired Outcome from Exercise 9.
• How close are you now to achieving your Desired Outcome on a scale of 1 to 10?
• Assuming that you are not yet at 10, jot down anything which prevents you being at 10, or anything which is still unsatisfactory that you hoped might have been resolved.
• Read through everything you wrote in Exercises 1 to 7 – notice anything which seems to be going well as well as things which are going not so well. Do you have an instinct about what the positive benefits of any of the negative aspects might be?
• Write the following headings across the top of a new page in your journal:

1	2	3		4	5
Replacements	CND	Positive intent		Positive Results	Negative Consequences
	(-)	(+)	=	(+)	(-)

• In column 2 write down any of the CNDs (Chronic Negative Deposits – chronic negative feelings such as fear, anger, bitterness, etc) from Exercise 5 which are still relevant.
• Sit quietly, read through your list of CNDs and ask yourself about each one, *What is the positive intention of holding on to this CND? Why is it important to me?*
Accept whatever answers you get, and then ask yourself, *What's important about that?* and so on, until you get to a bottom line (eg to get love and approval). Write your answers in column 3.
• Now look back at the CNDs and their positive intention, and in column 4 list the positive results of holding on to each CND.
• When you are satisfied with your list of positive results, gather the negative consequences of holding on to the CNDs in the same way. Write them column 5. Be sure to include the physical sensations that go with holding those CNDs.
• Look at the total equation and bottom line it in one sentence, ie *Holding on to (the major CND) keeps me, gives me or equals (the bottom line positive result).* (Look at some of the examples in Chapter Eight.)
• Look at the equation, and if you haven't already done so, find the illogicality of how you are trying to reach positive results, but going about it

negative way which is interfering with your aim to have a happy and productive life. Describe the CNDs to yourself in great detail (as if they belonged to someone else) and see how they do not give you the result you want. If you get a buzz (or burst into tears), you have found something that has been in your blind spot. Be confident that things can now start to change.

- Put a vertical line through columns 2 and 5, crossing out all the negative aspects. Circle the positive aspects of the intention and results that you want to maintain (eg security, learning, feeling good, getting attention, etc).
- Ask yourself what positive feeling(s) you would like or need to have which could replace each CND and give the same positive results. List the replacements in column 1 (eg 'unclear' is replaced by 'clarity', 'sadness' by 'joy', etc).

Decide whether you need some time to integrate this new learning, in which case, thank yourself for the work you have done today. Just notice over the next few days how your Unconscious Equation operates in your life and think about how it might be to change your pattern, how it would be to do things differently.

It isn't always easy to discover your Unconscious Equation working alone, so you may need to do this exercise over a period of days. Get what answers you can now, and give yourself permission to go on working on the questions and to have the answers come to your conscious awareness within the next week.

When you are ready to make a change, the first step is to sit down quietly wonder what part of you, in or around you, identifies with the Unconscious Equation. For whom has this been its way of being? What has been driving the behaviours? Where in you have you been holding the CNDs? Where do you feel them in your body? These questions will give you the places to begin looking, the doorways.

Over the next week or two, notice occasions when, out of habit, the old pattern begins, and when you begin to notice the benefits of the new option. When you are ready, work further on recovering the energy which has been devoted to this way of 'non-living', using the techniques in Exercise 14.

Exercise 18 Integrating 'I' and 'Me/Self'

Allow 30-45 minutes

Read through the whole exercise before you begin.

Get into a calm, quiet state. With eyes closed, say hello to yourself. At all stages, say thank you for any response you get.

Keeping your hands apart, rest them gently on your lap, palms up. Sense which hand holds 'I', and which holds 'Self'*. (You may prefer to use the word 'Me' instead of 'Self'.) Do this instinctively, but even if you feel you are guessing, trust that the guess comes from an educated place. As soon as you know which is which, ask the part of you that knows how to do this to please give you two visual representations or pictures, one of I and one of Self or Me. As soon as you have images, say 'Thank you'. Do not be concerned if you get an abstract picture symbolising you, or if you only get the sense of a picture, rather than a clear image. You can work with anything, and everything gets a 'thank you'.

Say 'hello' to each picture and thank it for being part of you and having whatever resources, attributes or positive characteristics it has.

There are now four distinct parts of you – the you of today sitting in the chair, the I image in one hand, the Self image in the other and the consciousness, the something in you which can see through your eyes and observe the two hands. Thank all four as they each have a specific role in what happens next. Continue to be respectful to everything that you see, feel and hear.

Addressing yourself to each hand in turn, ask questions aloud of I and Self. 'Listen' instinctively for any telepathic answers and speak them aloud. The parts will tend to answer you literally, and may not necessarily give the answers you expect. But that's the point. Accept the first thing you get. You are here to ask them and learn from these parts of yourself which are not normally in your conscious awareness.

Ask the following questions of each one.
- *I, do you know Self? Self, do you know I?* (Wait for both answers.)
- *I, can you see Self? Self, can you see I? Which way are you facing?* (Have them turn to face each other if need be.)
- *How old are you?* (Ask each in turn.)
- *Is one of you more masculine or feminine?*
- *In the last week, have you affected my life in some way? If so, how?*
- *Do you like each other?*
- *What sort of relationship do you have with each other?*

---

* This process of 'Self' and 'Other' communication, which is a foundation piece in the RAPSI model, originated with NLP (Neuro-Linguistic Programming).

- *What sort of relationship would you like to have with each other?*
- *What has been keeping you apart? What is there between you that has stopped you coming together before now?*
- *What wants do you have for yourself? And for the other?*
- *What resources do you each have?*
- *Each of you look into the other and say what attributes and resources you see in the other. Describe them. Each of you pick one attribute from the other that you wish you had had in the past.*

All you may have needed to do is to gather this information. If I and Self seem to be in harmony with one another and cooperating together in your life, you are ready to go to straight to the 'Scale holder' section.

If the relationship has not been good, you and they may need to dig a little. I or Self may be judging the other based on outward appearance (*You are slovenly and you hold me back. You are slave-driver and you don't know how to have fun.*) A step towards resolving this is to remind them of the attributes or resources the other has and that they would like – the 'driving I' might like the ability to relax, while the 'caring Self' might like the ability to speak honestly, for example. Tell them that when they merge, they will each have access to all that the other brings.

You will find they each have a monopoly on their particular attributes, eg confidence, expression, warmth, caring. If one does have all or most of an attribute, life may have been difficult for the other. To verify this ask each, *Please look at your life, from now back to childhood, and tell the other and me in the chair what it was like. What are your key memories, feelings and lasting impressions?*

You will notice that while they shared some or all of the same period of your life, their experiences can be quite different. This will build understanding between them and you (and the consciousness which is observing) and set up the first stage of building partnership, before moving on to integration. They can really begin to empathise with each other and with the effects that this has had on them and on you.

A new trial relationship

In some cases it may feel right to continue (in which case go to 'The Scale-holder'). Others of you may want to stop here to review what you have learned and to understand the implications of having this split in your system and how this may have stopped you achieving your Desired Outcome(s). If so, then think about how integrating these two would bring new harmony into your life, having the best of both. Before you stop, get agreement from the two aspects of yourself that they will work together to support you in the coming week or fortnight. (Aim to complete the next part of the process as soon as possible to ensure that this interim arrangement does not become a new structure which you have to rediscover.) Ask each part how specifically they will support you, eg *I will help you speak out in meetings. I will help you be more caring.*

You of today then promises to make contact with them (in your mind's eye), at least twice a day, first thing in the morning and last thing at night, to check how they are, learn from them, ask their advice, and maintain the link. You might even have deliberate 'planning sessions' with them: *What shall I say in this report? What do you think of this decision I am about to make? How can I solve this problem with my son?* Review the events with them afterwards.

If you have learned that one or both of them has an apparently negative or restrictive job (eg *I stop you speaking clearly at meetings*), say 'thank you' and ask: *What is the positive intention of your job?*

It may be something like: *To keep you quiet.* Keep asking *And what's important about that?* until you get your bottom line answer (see page 34), which may be *To keep you quiet – so that you go unnoticed – so you don't look foolish – to keep you safe – so you feel good.* Very quickly both you (in the chair) and the aspect of you will realise that you and it are not getting the positive outcome that you want. The actual result seems to be: *I don't speak clearly in meetings so I get flustered, others think I'm a fool and I'm passed over for promotion, so I feel bad!*

Ask the observer, I and Self how to generate other ways of achieving the bottom line outcome. Choose the one which is most beneficial to you. Then ask both I and Self parts how they will support you in achieving this.

Note that you are starting to develop your 'cheering section', your support group. Develop this relationship as a first step towards integration and learn from it.

Thank all four parts of you for the work you have done so far.

The Scale-holder

If you are starting work again after a break, make your usual preparations before you continue.

When you first had I and Self look at each other, you asked them what had been keeping them apart. Some of the typical answers to this question are, *There's a wall between us, a gap, a line, a force field. I can see Self, but Self cannot see I, there's a one-way mirror.*

There is a positive intention why something is maintaining the split and that something needs to be found.

After several clients had discovered that one hand holding I or Self was lighter or heavier than the other and that something was holding them in balance, we recognised the reality of the scales and a scale-holder (see Chapter 11). The one who observes (the 'fourth part' we talked about earlier) and has the job of maintaining the split may wish to be called something else in your system, (judge, Dad, controller, etc) but for now it's Scale-holder. Here are a few ways

of discovering who this is.
- Ask who is keeping I and Self apart.
- Have I and Self look into your head and body and see who or what is doing this job.
- Feel where the scale-holder might reside.
- Follow the wall/gap/line and see where it goes.

Once you find Scale-holder, ask it all the usual questions, especially finding its positive attributes and positive intention). Your aim is to have it see that whatever it is trying to achieve on your behalf (some form of protection) is no longer appropriate and is probably not working. Discover which part it has been favouring, 'right' or 'left'? Enable it to understand that it is important that both parts work together. Find out what alternative job it would like to do towards your Desired Outcome (it is probably not up-to-date, so tell it what you want for yourself). As soon as it has understood its new positive role, you can move to checking your future vision.

Future vision

In Exercise 11 you found your Future Self and brought in the energy of your future and your past. This next part of the exercise will deepen the integration.

Have I, Self and Stake-holder show you how they will combine their positive attributes to create your future. See your Future with their contribution. It may look the same as the one you created from your Desired Outcome, but richer, or possibly beyond your previous expectations. Thank each of the three again. You are ready to move to integration. Having done all the preliminary work, this should be becoming easier.

Integration

Your aim is to find light in I, Self, Scale-holder and the rest of you and to integrate all the light/energy, radiating all through you and outwards – and to bring back in the energy of the future that you just saw.

First find the light in I and Self by looking into the images and through any layers of colour or form until you find pure or translucent light. If one is well lit but the other seems dim or lacking in energy, the one with light can send some of its light to the other, which usually helps free the light in the other.

Now have those two lights see the light in the Scale-holder and in the rest of you. Have all the lights see and say hello to each other.

Help each light to radiate (the form may disappear and you may only be sense/seeing light), invite the three sources of light energy to come together in you as follows: Raise both hands, palms up, so that your elbows are also raised. Give permission for the lights to come together and as you watch this happen (in your mind's eye), feel your hands following, closing the gap. Allow this process to happen naturally and as slowly or as quickly as it needs to. You may feel deeply within your body as this integration begins to happen. As the

170

light energies meet and mingle, allow your hands to come together. Then pause. When you feel ready to bring the energy fully into your body, notice which seems to be the right place into which to bring your united energy (heart, chest, stomach, mouth, etc) and let your hands go there and feel the energy infuse you and radiate. Sit quietly and allow the integration to continue until it feels right to stop.

Open your eyes and note down what you learned, what you now feel. The effects of the integration can be immediate or can take a few hours or days to assimilate as your new-found harmony works its way though your life.

If during this basic sequence you discover additional parts or layers as you do this work, acknowledge and thank them, and then investigate them in the same way you investigated I and Self, looking through the layers until you reach the light which you then help to radiate. Then continue with the work you were doing originally. If for whatever reason you have to leave some parts 'unresolved', then simply promise them that you will come back when you can give them the time they need for acknowledgement and release.

Keep that promise!

Thank yourself and your system for doing this significant piece of work.

Take as long as you like.

Exercise 19 Having it all

Your life works up to a point, you get by, but why not be 'greedy'? Here are some things to look for in your life that are indications of trapped energy. If any of them applies to you, use the three questions as the starting point for finding your doorway – and then follow the RAPSI 5R process. The other exercises and the case studies throughout the book will give you clues about approaches you might take if things don't follow the straightforward pattern – and they won't!

Remember that the most important thing you do is to acknowledge everything that communicates with you and thank it for its positively-intended communication – however much you might feel that you want to ignore it, suppress it or get rid of it!

I feel that I don't deserve things. It is greedy to want too much!
- *Whose familiar voice is saying that?*
- *Where is that voice coming from?*
- *How much of me on a scale of 1 to 10 is fully living? How much is not and thought it didn't deserve to live fully?*

Tension headaches and places of stress.
- *Where do I feel this?*
- *What is going on in my life when I feel this?*
- *Name one apparently positive result I get from this happening.*

Late for appointments and/or procrastination.
- *What in me is holding back, is distracted or is afraid to commit?*
- *Where does that exist inside or outside my body?*
- *What positive result(s), if any, arise(s) from this?*

Pushing yourself, feeling pressured.
- *What in me is driving me, pushing me, pressuring me?*
- *Where from?*
- *What would it get if I did everything it wants me to do?*

I'm allergic to ..., put off by ..., I run away from ...
- *What do I fear will happen if I don't react this way?*
- *If part of me was running away, where is it running to and what's there?*
- *If I was holding something inside my body and/or keeping something outside, what is it and what's important about that?*

I always want what I can't have, I seem permanently frustrated.
- *What was the earliest moment in my life that I did I not have what I wanted?*
- *What in me feels it is not worthy of, allowed to, or able to have what it wants?*
- *Where do I hold the frustration? What does it want, from whom and what would be evidence that it got it?*

I can barely hide my jealousy and competitiveness.
- *What age in me is speaking?*
- *When was I superceded by another?*
- *Where does the speaker speak from?*

I am always trying to catch up with myself.
- *Where is my future in relation to my body? Point to it.*
- *Who or what is out in my future and do they know I exist?*
- *What would I and they gain and lose if they joined me in the present?*

My relationships don't work. I blame them.
- *How good is my relationship with myself?*
- *What do I think of myself?*
- *What in me does the blaming?*

I worry about ...
- *Where in me do I worry from?*
- *If I learned to worry from someone else, who was it?*
- *Where in or around me do I hold them?*

I feel overly responsible for ...
- *How young was I when I took responsibility for others, for events?*
- *What do I get (positively) from feeling overly responsible?*
- *What do I want to feel instead?*

I blush, I feel shy, I have difficulty socialising.

- *How much of me on a scale of 1 to 10 is present in my handshake?*
- *How much of me is out in front, visible? How much is inside hiding?*
- *If I were more visible, what do I fear most?*

I feel confused a lot of the time, I can't make up my mind.
- *What is it I fear would happen if I were clear and could decide?*
- *What might be the positive intention of holding on to confusion?*
- *If I could make up my mind, what would be different?*

I don't trust many people.
- *When, who and what caused me not to trust? When, if ever, did I trust?*
- *What in me is not trusting others and where does it reside?*
- *What part of me don't I trust, is untrustworthy?*

I keep banging my right knee, having accidents, breaking things.
- *What is my knee trying to tell me?*
- *On a scale of 1 to 10, how much of me is in my body? Where is the rest of me?*
- *If not all of me is paying attention, what is it focusing on?*

Now think of other statements which summarise how you may be living your life below par. What similar questions might you ask yourself? What else are you curious to find out?

Exercise 20 Integrating the observers

Allow up to an hour

Before you do anything else, set up two chairs facing one another, then sit in one of them. Read Chapter Eleven which will help you to detect, through language, feelings and behaviour patterns, the observers in your energetic system, the bits of you which stay judging, watching, sceptical, doubting and controlling. Read the exercise right through before starting the work.

Given that their intention has been to help you to stay safe, or retain your identity, your observers are usually pretty adept at staying separate and unknown. Also it may be the 'you' you've always been, and you've simply never had the opportunity to look at yourself. So how do you work with this? Well the first thing to realise is that whatever helps you explore your system is probably an observer and it may need now to finally look for itself. For this reason, we cannot just give you recipes to follow. It is time to engage with the fundamentals of your belief system and some major elements of your energetic structure. When you are locating the key observers, you are working with the very building blocks of your energetic structure and the final pieces, which will enable you to achieve wholeness. You will be voyaging into new territory. Trust your system and see how far it will take you. Trust also that your system will only take you as far as is right for you in this situations, at this time.

What follows are some suggestions that you can try for yourself and we invite feedback on how far you have been able to go. Then it's up to you to get curious, incorporate everything you have learnt so far and enjoy the journey!

- Re-read your Unconscious Equation from Exercise 17. Locate it by noticing what you feel, in or around your body, as you think of it.
- Pay special attention to what you fear you might lose by having your Desired Outcome. If it comes down to identity (the 'not-you' identity), who is holding that identity now? Where does this exist in your energetic structure?
- Pay attention to the pictures you make. If you notice that you are seeing endless colours, scenes and taking endless journeys, but not really resolving things, there is probably a 'picture maker'. Where does it look from? From where does it project its pictures? How old is it? What's its positive intention?
- If you keep doubting yourself, others and this process, you have an issue of trust and you may be wedded to a negative scenario, or doubting so that you are not disappointed. This is a fundamental pattern, learnt young, and that younger you may be looking out through your eyes, knowing nothing about you. Perhaps it knows a lot about this world but is staying in a false security, existing, not living.
- If something says, *I will only come in when you are ready, when you are*

pure, when you have cleaned up your act, etc, it does not realise that until it comes in, you will never be ready, you will never be pure, you will never be able to clean up your act fully. It's time for the observer's energy to 'come on down' from on high or 'come on in' from outside to help you make this possible. Clearly, just trying to pull its light through you is not going to work until you have a new joint agreement and have woken up a locationally higher or distant energy to the plight of its vehicle, you, on the planet.

- If you hold strong beliefs that keep something separate from you - a witness, a deity, guides, other beings, the place of silence, etc, – you are probably creating false idols. Whatever we invest our energy in – to give us comfort or to reflect back to us greater knowledge or the promise of salvation, or a partial peace – takes energy on our part to maintain. It keeps at a distance the very energy and light which those beliefs are designed to deliver. That wisdom, that great love out there is ours, it is you, and anything that keeps you from you needs integrating. What in you holds those beliefs? Where or who did they come from? Where do you hold those outer energies?

- If you are a really nice person and you have come to believe your own PR, the last thing that you want to face is that there is something that feels 'nasty' inside, that you have a dark place that you have covered over and forgotten. Look into all your dark corners for 'treasure' and for light. Remember to look below your feet to find the energies in the earth. The good news is that whatever you find that is dark is the most compressed condition of white light energy, and it is holding light. The 'shadow' can and needs to be penetrated and light released. Keeping dark in order to see light is the old paradigm. Finding and radiating all light is the new paradigm. So look for the dark spaces, remember to thank them for their protective jobs,.

- If you find this wonderful patch of dark in the back of the head but each time you try to look into it, you drift off to sleep, you may have found a void, the deep velvety black, which protects a vastness of light. Try the chair exercise below as a way of probing it.

- If you know that you control yourself, but you just cannot seem to locate your controller, it may be because it keeps looking somewhere else for itself! Again the chair exercise below might be helpful.

Move chairs

Sit in the chair opposite where you have just been sitting and from that position, keeping your outer eyes open (to help you maintain a dissociated position), look back and see (sense/see) yourself sitting where you were before. Say hello to 'yourself' in the original chair, get 'yourself' to say hello to the 'you' now doing the exploring.

Look into the depths of 'yourself' (as you have done in previous exercises). Look into the area where you think that you may have located an observer – try looking through and out behind, above and below, inside and outside the body. Who or what is there? (The observer may take any form.) When you find who or what it is, say hello and invite them to see 'you', the explorer. This can be a powerful moment of realisation that time has moved on and that you have the body and are the 'home' that the observer's energy finally needs to come into.

This is time for a real conversation, so put down the step-by-step guide book. What do you need to say to each other? What do you need to understand each from the other? What do you fear might be lost when you become one being?

There will be loss, it is time to mourn those old friends who may have been with your through lifetimes: anger, hurt, pain, old limiting patterns. It is time to welcome new feelings of peace, joy, satisfaction, fulfilment, calm, vibrancy and aliveness so that this is what you are radiating.

We cannot guide you, because without your detail what we say will be meaningless. Trust your instincts. Be with, empathise with, relate to your observer self and then when you are both ready, find the light in the observer and have that light see the light in You the explorer. Find any and all light in or around 'you' and help it to flood 'you' until you are fully 'lit'. Then, when it seems right, walk back to the first chair, sit down and feel the completion. Feel the energy expand and tingle through your body. Feel the heat as you radiate and your energy expands into the room, the house, the street, the town, the county, the universe. And, if you have achieved this, know that this fundamental feeling will last.

And if something crops up to disrupt it? It simply means that you are very close to completion and simply have another observer to find.

Otherwise, you are fully here. Congratulations!

Please congratulate yourself.

Afterword

This book is the result of 25 years of experience working with clients, capturing the emerging and unfolding universal journey of the light to know itself, a tale of fragmentation and unification of energy.

What I have learned surpasses even the far-reaching questions I knew to ask and wonder about in the early days. What I am left with is an understanding of the universal patterns of

- dis-ease within the human condition,
- humankind's progress in a sequential process of evolvement, as energy, through lifetimes, and as a multi-dimensional system.

And arising from these

- a method of facilitation to help complete the process of becoming whole and a model of grounded spirituality.

The fragmented self has been signalling the need for integration. As we look around the globe at the human condition, at the lack of Recognition, at poor Relationships, at the need for Reconciliation, it is clear that the final two 'Rs', Release of positive energy and Radiance, are sorely missing, hidden beyond the violence of both people and nature.

There is an old saying 'darkest before dawn'. Our task with RAPSI is to enable people to bring forth the light/energy from its own darkness, its historical protection.

As you have journeyed through these pages, you have been touched by your own sense of truth and wisdom and have been enabled to begin or accelerate the process towards full 'R&R' – Release and Radiance!

The Missing Peace

Peace begins within. It then reflects itself back from the external universe, the world. It is achievable. It is desirable. The key to its achievement is discovering the code (like a combination on a safe) that unlocks our fragmented structure towards the unification of split consciousness, a state of integrated being, wholeness, authenticity. The more people that take this universal journey, the more people who unify themselves, the more beacons of light there will be to shine and be the example, creating a groundswell, a positive contagion, a wave of creative power which heals wounds and creates positive connections and a positive world. This is the beginning of the END – the Evolutionary New Dawning. It is an exciting time in history as it is time for the next steps in this stage of human development and evolvement, which will enable each of us to empower ourselves fully, to become a power for good.

Our mission, which has stimulated the writing of this book, is to help transform 'negative' energy on the planet, so that more people are radiating, fully helping to bring in a complete shift in consciousness and create the missing peace. We know that we are not alone in this endeavour and the fact that you have picked up the book and read this far suggests that you are treading a similar path. Thank you for being a kindred spirit and for entrusting us with a part of your journey as you travelled along with us and our clients, in this book, and explored your inner space.

Eileen Watkins Seymour

Acknowledgements

It is normal to want to acknowledge those who have helped in some way with the creation of a book. Since this book represents my life's work, my acknowledgements too span the experience of my life to date – 60 years' worth.

Unsurprisingly it begins with my mother, a courageous 'lifer' who taught me many things. The writing of this book is an example of 'where there's a will, there's a way'. Dad's legacy to me was 'think', and I took that seriously as I pondered the questions of well being, health, dis-ease and the possibility of there being universal patterns. I honour too my dear children, Marc and Sharon, my barometer, my joy and my pride. Thank you for your endurance through times of change, for your unflagging trust and for your love.

I acknowledge all my teachers from the early years through university and beyond.

I honour my husbands: David Watkins, a thoughtful man of achievement who helped broaden my experience of life, bringing me and our children to England, to the start of a new life, and enabling me to undertake further studies in order to pursue my career as a psychotherapist; Jonathan Seymour Jr for his cheerful support for myself and my children as I helped birth NLP in the UK in the early 80s; and of course I thank Clive Digby-Jones for his continual unconditional love, for staunchly supporting and being part of my dream to share the understandings and knowledge that I've gained during this and possibly other lifetimes, and for helping me express this in writing, in teaching and in facilitating others.

I thank all the great thinkers, explorers, scientists, philosophers, inventors through time, all those with a burning curiosity to discover the secrets of the universe and the keys to open them, who inspired me in my formative years and today.

Nearer the present I pay tribute to all the co-developers of the NLP technology, which has positively touched many lives around the world and which stimulated me to begin exploring the internal universe. Special thanks go to Gene Early, who helped inspire my desire to start an NLP movement in the UK and who was instrumental in helping Graham Dawes (huge thanks!) and myself create the UK Training Centre for NLP. So much learning. So many experiences of change and growth.

Thanks also for special moments … Robert Dilts, David Gordon, Dave Dobson, Barbara Witney, and the late David Gaster. You helped provide ground-breaking quality trainings.

There were so many others through the years, too many to list. But thanks to you all. Each of you left your mark.

I also want to thank every participant who took our NLP programmes (1979-1987) and then during the RAPSI years. You were part of my experience and my learning, helping me to expand my understanding of how to find and engage with inner space and begin to affect limiting patterns of behaviour – my own and other people's.

RAPSI would not have been developed without my clients. It was each of you who provided the jewels in the crown of my learning. It was you who answered questions that no-one but myself challenged me to hold. It was you who, through time, provided me with answers to questions that most people do not know to ask. It was your problems, your explorations, your discoveries and your allowing me to be fully with you, helping me guide you, that drove my curiosity to the limits and beyond. You are the pioneers. My thanks and my indebtedness for finding your way to my door.

And today, thank you to the RAPSI graduates, deeply motivated to grow, learn and contribute. You are helping to sharpen our learning as we teach and some of you are becoming the new generation of teachers and facilitators.

Finally, a big thank you to my dear friend Susan Norman, without whom this book would still be a virtual anticipated reality – and to Hugh L'Estrange for his invaluable part in the publishing process.

And to Reinhard Kowalski, Consultant Clinical Psychologist, who spoke the words 'you have the missing piece', which triggered the title of this book: *The Missing Peace.*

What clients have said about RAPSI

The Ravenscroft Approach (to psycho-spiritual integration) goes significantly beyond NLP in technique and theory, in that it focuses not on the relatively superficial structure of the mind and its modelling, but attends to the deep energetic infrastructure of consciousness and a wholistic technique of unifying the mind's fragmented consciousness.

Dr Greg Hitter, PhD, clinical psychologist and author

RAPSI is the missing piece that connects energy and matter. The process uses words, but always tries to go beyond the rigid boundaries of words, to connect with the energy behind them. In a way, all psychotherapy aims to do this, but usually gets stuck in the words, never going beyond the story-mind. The missing piece is to use words to go beyond themselves.

Reinhard Kowalski, author, consultant clinical psychologist, practising psychotherapist, Associate Fellow of the British Psychological Society

It has changed my understanding of healing; I have experienced healing which I had not thought was possible on this side of the grave. Certain wounds are healed now as I explore new landscapes of the soul using RAPSI techniques. No longer is healing a cessation of physical, mental or emotional symptoms, only for them to reappear in another guise elsewhere. It is a healing of the spirit.

Dr Adele Markovic MBChb and RAPSI Practitioner

Surprisingly simple and effective. A great weight that I've been carrying all my life has lifted. I can't believe it. What can I say? I feel completely different and yet the same. The real me.

Sarah Zimin, Educator and author

One of the most powerful pieces of changework that I use in the London Shyness Centre.

Lynne Crawford, Therapist, healer and author

Clive & Eileen have opened up the Fast Track to effective change. … I believe that leadership starts with managing yourself and they showed me how.

Alan Sears, Motivational speaker and author

At last! I have been waiting for your book for over 20 years. One-to-one sessions with you have helped me shape my life and create who I am today. To have even a fragment of your wisdom, perception, knowledge and understanding of the human psyche contained in the book, to which I can always have instant access, to dip into as I wish, will be truly invaluable.

Liz Sutcliffe, Entrepreneur, one of Eileen's early clients

Before I began to work with you, I had no idea of even the concept of what you were doing; although I thought I did! You turned my 'spiritual construct' inside out. There is no way I would have got there, just doing and believing what I did and believed! Thank you! Now I know what 'I AM' really means! How amazing is that?

PS I work a lot in the Native American Tradition and what you do is true soul-retrieval.

Ann Whittle, Educator and author

The love you have given me and others on the training has been amazing and the work you do is truly life changing. Thank you for your love and genius.

Philip Clarke, Cranial-Sacral Osteopath and RAPSI graduate

RAPSI is an excellent addition to reflexology. You've changed my life.

Sandra Weston, Reflexologist and RAPSI Practitioner

Although this book was written by three people, 'we' always refers to Eileen and Clive.

All the cases studies are accounts of actual sessions with clients of Eileen and/or Clive. Names and some details have been changed to protect anonymity. The exceptions are where Eileen, Clive or Susan explicitly refer to their own experiences.

Index

Contact

*Eileen Watkins Seymour, BA MA Studies in Humanistic Psychology, DSc (HC),
is a UKCP registered psychotherapist, healer & leadership coach. A pioneer, first
as a teacher in the US, introducing new ideas to the classroom as part of the
human potential movement in the 60s, then moving to the UK and co-founding
the first NLP centre in Europe. Through client work in private practice, she
developed RAPSI – The Ravenscroft Approach to psycho-spiritual intergration. She
is married to Clive and has two children. Although she has previously published
articles about her work, The Missing Peace is her first book.*

*Clive Digby-Jones is a corporate facilitator, leadership coach and healer. With a
background in business management, he held board positions up to MD and non-
executive director. As Innovation Consultant, he studied Walt Disney for the Disney
Corporation and developed trainings in creativity and the process of innovation. As
co-developer, he writes about and teaches RAPSI and presents the material in the
media. He is married to Eileen and has four children.*

Eileen and Clive are happy to stage introductory empowerment workshops
(The Missing Peace), give talks, offer training for established practitioners and
healers and those wishing to gain skills in RAPSI. Currently, they see clients in
London (East Finchley) and in South Bucks (Ibstone), and are willing to travel
throughout the UK and to other countries.

They also work in the corporate field, offering Awakening Workshops, Energy
Audit, the Step-Change Programme, Intensives, Leadership Development and
Executive Coaching, and they have experience in facilitating company boards
to define their strategic direction, achieve board and senior management
alignment, and implement strategic innovation programmes. Contact through:
success@leadershipgroup.co.uk or www.rapsi.org

*Susan Norman is a teacher, teacher trainer and author who has written more
than 30 books, mostly on language teaching. With Hugh L'Estrange (her partner
in business and life), she owns Saffire Press, which has published her two books on
NLP for teaching and learning and SEAL approaches. Susan and Hugh are also
Co-Directors of the leading-edge learning organisation, SEAL (Society for Effective
Affective Learning). She can be contacted through the SEAL website:
www.seal.org.uk*